The Lizard Keeper's Handbook

Philippe de Vosjoli

Table of Contents

Introduction

Insect-eating (insectivorous) lizards, an arbitrary grouping based on dietary preference, account for a great majority of the more than 3,800 recognized species of lizards. They comprise one of the most successful groups of vertebrates, having evolved great variety of forms and adaptations, and colonized a wide diversity of habitats. Indeed, in many areas insect-eating lizards are extremely abundant, accounting for a significant percentage of the animal biomass. Because of this relative abundance, several species of insect-eating lizards are collected and sold by the thousands annually in the pet trade. With proper management, which should include establishing collecting seasons for respective species and annual quotas based on field studies, many of the populations of insect-eating lizards have a high recovery rate and are good candidates for sustained field culture. The current philosophy in herpetoculture strives towards establishing viable self-sustaining captive-breeding populations through managed field culture and/ or through more controlled systems of indoor and outdoor vivaria. A number of lizard species, such as some of the geckos, bearded dragons, and more recently veiled chameleons, have proven very adaptable and economical to breed in large numbers in captivity.

Generally, lizards that are easy to maintain in captivity are those species which are the most adaptable to the relatively simple setups and limited diets provided by most keepers. Species that are very specialized, either in terms of their environmental requirements or in terms of their dietary needs, require a much closer duplication of those conditions and requirements in order to survive in captivity. Because of the diversity of adaptations and consequent requirements of insect-eating lizards, any prospective lizard keeper will need to acquire a sound base of information on lizard husbandry, as well as basic information on the particular species to be kept. A lizard maintained under the wrong conditions and offered the wrong diet cannot survive for very long in captivity.

The purpose of this book is to give herpetoculturists, both beginners and those more experienced, as well as pet industry personnel, a broad base of knowledge which will allow them to successfully keep a variety of insect-eating lizards. Although the emphasis of this book is on husbandry, all herpetoculturists should strive to captive-breed the species they keep. This helps to provide important information on the captive-breeding and -rearing of a wide variety of species; it also plays an important part in assuring that these species remain available for years to come. Remember: Species that are inexpensive and readily available today can become valuable, rare, and highly-in-demand in the future. As a herpetoculturist, opportunities for acquiring an important base of knowledge abound. Indeed, relatively little is known of the life history, social behaviors, husbandry requirements and reproduction of the great major-ity of lizards. A continually improved base of knowledge, combined with the involvement of herpetoculturists, could one day play a critical role in the conservation of many of these species.

Note: Because herpetoculture is rapidly expanding, new infor-mation is becoming available every year. Some of this informa-tion will make a significant portion of our current knowledge obsolete. Ongoing research on lizard diets and nutrition will result in new approaches to feeding lizards and insects and in the development of better vitamin/mineral supplements. Work is also currently being conducted toward developing lighting which generates enough UV-B to (hypothetically) affect vita-min D3 synthesis. Because of this rapidly changing base of knowledge, this manual will be revised over the years to include updated information.

Obtaining Information

One cannot overemphasize the need to acquire information when considering the keeping of insect-eating lizards or any kind of reptile. Keeping lizards is _very_ different from keeping dogs, cats or birds, and considerably more attention needs to be given to environmental and dietary factors. Although this book offers methods for determining the requirements of most insect-eating lizards, whenever possible one should strive to obtain accurate species-specific information.

But I Can't Find any Information on This Lizard I Just Bought!

There is now a wealth of literature on reptiles available from book dealers and specialized reptile stores, though lack of information used to be a widespread problem encountered by many herpetoculturists. The first step is to obtain as much information as possible from the seller at the time of purchase, especially the correct name of the animal and its country of origin. Whenever possible, obtain the scientific name of the animal. Common names of reptiles in the pet trade may have little resemblance to the names used by herpetologists and may end up confusing your search for information. Because exporters are required to list animals by scientific name, this information is usually available, although the scientific names may sometimes be inaccurate or outdated. Fortunately, listing animals by their scientific names has become standard procedure in the mail order reptile business.

Once one learns the scientific name and the country or area of origin, one can examine books in a pet store and check the subjects and indexes to find out if information is available on that particular animal. Some publishers, including Advanced Vivarium Systems, produce species- or family-specific books which can provide most of the basic information on husbandry that you will need. If no information is available on specific husbandry, books on the natural history of reptiles, field guides and books on herpetology can provide useful information which may allow you to determine an animal's requirements. Although only a few specialized reptile dealers have an extensive selection of the herpetological works available, there are many mail order natural history book dealers offering a good

Many specialized reptile stores carry a wide selection of both herpetocultural and herpetological literature.

selection of reptile-related literature. Check herpetocultural publications such as *The Vivarium, Amphibian & Reptile Magazine, Reptiles,* and herpetological society newsletters for sources. A few of the larger herpetological societies also sell a wide selection of herpetological books.

If one cannot locate useful information in those sources, it can often be found in the herpetological publications and books available at a local university library, particularly one with a herpetology department. Another course is to search through scientific literature. Going to a university library and consulting the *Zoological Record,* as far back as twenty years, often produces potentially valuable references. Librarians can provide assistance in helping you learn to use the *Zoological Record.* Once obtained, these sources of information, i.e., scientific articles, will yield additional sources if one consults the references mentioned by an article's author.

Common sense

One problem with literature research is that it takes time. Because time may often be a critical factor with a newly obtained species, common sense often plays an important role in initially designing a vivarium and determining a dietary regimen. One approach would be to examine the form of an animal for clues as to its habits. As an example, many flattened lizards are rock dwellers. Laterally flattened lizards with long tails are usually arboreal. The long tails provide stability for arboreal lizards when climbing and resting on branches. Lizards with vertical pupils are crepuscular (active around dawn and dusk), or nocturnal (active at night), while lizards with round pupils are usually diurnal (active during the daylight hours). Lizards with flattened snouts (shovel-nose appearance), smooth, very shiny scales and reduced limbs are often fossorial (they bury in substrate). Lizards with toe pads, such as geckos and anoles, are climbing lizards; they climb on bark, rock, plants, etc. With experience, one learns to take cues from a lizard's appearance and behavior when assessing its requirements.

When in doubt, the easiest way to assess a lizard's requirements is to design a vivarium rich in topographical and microclimatological diversity. When a lizard is introduced into this type of environment it usually chooses what it prefers. This type of vivarium should include a variety of shelters, climbing areas, substrates, temperature range, humidity and light. By observing the lizard's behavior, you should be able to determine its preferences. Remember that some lizards, particularly species from mountain areas, may require cooler temperatures, so allow for a cool gradient in an experimental vivarium if you suspect you may have such a species.

You may also want to experiment with diet. Several species of insect-eating lizards (day geckos, veiled chameleons, bearded dragons and swifts) also eat some plant material and/or baby foods. Others may feed on non-living foods, such as a lean canned dog food or fine strips of beef heart or chopped boiled chicken. These may include many of the small teiids and skinks, some of the larger agamines, some of the lacertids, small monitors, etc. Lizards that are frequent tongue flickers often feed on non-living food. Your observation and experimentation will prove to be the best sources of information for determining your lizard's preferences. As long as an animal is healthy at the time of purchase or collection, you should have enough time to determine its requirements by experimentation. Remember, what non-specialized or inexperienced pet store personnel tell you can often be wrong.

Illustration by Kevin Anderson.

BEFORE BUYING
INSECT-EATING LIZARDS

Several factors should be considered before buying insect-eating lizards. Many first-time buyers make initial errors in selection that eventually result in disappointment or failure.

Who are the lizards for?

Are the lizards for you or for your children? Except for the larger, easily handled species, insect-eating lizards are not recommended for children unless their parents can provide close supervision. Parents must be willing to assume responsibility and supervision for proper maintenance and handling. Although lizards should not be considered children's pets, they are highly recommended for responsible adolescents.

Do you want a lizard as a display or as a pet that can be handled?

If regular handling is a consideration, then inquire about species that have an established reputation as pets, such as bearded dragons (*Pogona vitticeps*) or Sudan plated lizards (*Gerrhosaurus major*). Leopard geckos (*Eublepharis macularius*) and African fat-tail geckos (*Hemitheconyx caudicinctus*) can also be handled on occasion; however, the great majority of insect-eating lizards are best considered primarily for display. There are other lizards outside of the insect-eating group, such as green iguanas, Australian blue-tongue skinks and some of the monitors which are better candidates for a relatively high level of human interaction.

Avoid buying on impulse.

Do a little research or reading on the species you are considering buying. Many impulse buyers are sorry later when they realize they can't readily accommodate the needs of their animal or the animal doesn't meet their expectations. Also, their animal may not fare well, become ill and die. Many impulse buyers of horned lizards, true chameleons or some of the Chilean lizards have been discouraged because they were unaware that these species tend to be difficult to keep in captivity.

Be willing to bear the cost of the appropriate setup.
Many people considering the purchase of a lizard for the first time will attempt to save money on essentials, such as a proper-size enclosure or adequate heating and lighting. Actually, you will find the cost of a vivarium is usually several times the cost of the animal(s) you are purchasing. This is the same cost relationship one encounters with the tropical fish hobby.

Is feeding going to be a problem?
You must also consider whether you will be able to adequately and regularly feed the animal(s) you purchase. With insect-eating lizards, this usually means a once-a-week trip to a local pet store, raising your own insects or having them delivered by mail-order. Take into account the time it takes for proper maintenance of these lizards.

Sex selection
If you are considering buying a single lizard, generally a male is preferable to a female. In the author's experience, male insect-eating lizards tend to live longer in captivity than females. In addition, females without males will not be given the opportunity to breed. If they are not bred when they are ovulating, they may have an increased chance of becoming egg-bound. The wisest decision would be to buy a sexual pair or a trio (one male, two females) when possible, and to provide your animals with the opportunity to reproduce.

Understanding Store Selections of Lizards
Many non-specialized, relatively inexperienced pet stores base their lizard selections more on low cost than on how well specific lizards will fare in captivity. This was the case with several of the Chilean lizards imported in recent years. They were inexpensive and pretty, yet seldom survived more than a few months. Many pet store personnel lack basic knowledge and often try to minimize losses with a focus on cheap wild-collected species. Unfortunately, inexperienced customers may want to save money and thus may select an inexpensive wild-collected species that will not fare well. It cannot be emphasized enough: Do your homework before you buy a lizard. There are specialized stores with personnel who know reptiles well; they can help you select a species that meets your specific needs. There are also many good books available and herpeto-culturists who are willing to share their knowledge.

Captive-bred versus wild-caught

Captive-bred lizards generally fare considerably better than wild-caught lizards because they are less likely to be infested with parasites or have diseases. Indeed, captive-bred lizards which have been established over several generations have a proven history of adapting to captivity. Unfortunately, relatively few species of insect-eating lizards are currently bred on a large commercial scale. Of these, the best known is the leopard gecko *(Eublepharis macularius)*, possibly the easiest of all lizards to keep in captivity. The Australian inland bearded dragon *(Pogona vitticeps)*, a delightful and personable species, is now being bred in increasing numbers (a few thousand annually) and its availability is expected to increase. Though bearded dragons are somewhat delicate as hatchlings, subadults and adults tend to fare well. Efforts are also being made to captive breed the veiled chameleon from Yemen *(Chamaeleo calyptratus)* on a large scale. There are many other species of insect-eating lizards that are bred on a small scale, including many kinds of geckos, basilisks and water dragons.

The mortality of wild-collected lizards is high, particularly with species requiring specialized environments and/or diets. If you are just starting out with lizards, select species that are known to establish well in captivity. Starting out with difficult species often results in failure which might discourage you from further pursuing the fascinating field of herpetoculture.

A New Caledonian prehensile-tailed gecko *(Rhacodactylus auriculatus)*. Members of this genus are among the most sought after of the captive-bred geckos. They feed on soft sweet fruit and insects.

Some Recommended Insect-Eating Lizards

Geckos (Families Eublepharidae and Gekkonidae): Over all, this diverse group of lizards (more than 900 species) is very adaptable to captivity and more species in this family are captive-bred than in any other. Some of the terrestrial species and tropical forest species can be delicate and may need specialized care. Some geckos rank among the most beautiful of lizards; others have bizarre and interesting forms. Their eyes are some of the most remarkable in the animal world. Among popular favorites there are leopard geckos *(Eublepharis macularius)*, African fat-tailed geckos *(Hemitheconyx)*, day geckos *(Phelsuma)*, tokay geckos *(Gecko gecko)*, flying geckos *(Ptychozoon)*, prehensile-tailed geckos *(Rhacodactylus)* and frog-eyed geckos *(Teratoscincus)*.

Agamine lizards (Family Chameleonidae; subfamily Agaminae): No generalizations can be made about agamine lizards; they comprise a very diverse group. Some species are very adaptable to captivity, such as inland bearded dragons *(Pogona vitticeps)*, the clown agamas of the pet trade *(Laudakia stellio brachydactyla)* and green water dragons *(Physignathus cocincinus)*. Others species, such as members of the genera *Gonocephalus, Draco,* and *Calotes,* are best recommended for specialists. Some species are difficult, such as toad-head agamas *(Phrynocephalus)* and several species in the genus *Agama*.

True chameleons (Family Chamaeleonidae; subfamily Chamaeleoninae): Most species are best considered moderately-to-highly difficult to keep in captivity. In fact, the longevity of many species in the wild is actually quite short. However, the veiled chameleon from Yemen*(Chamaeleo calyptratus)* has proven very adaptable to captivity and is now being bred in increasing numbers by herpetoculturists in the United States. The panther chameleon from Madagascar *(Chamaeleo pardalis)* has also proven quite adaptable. *Bradypodion thamnobates,* a dwarf live-bearing South African species introduced in herpetoculture by world renowned expert, Bert Langerwerf, may turn out to be one of the very best chameleons to keep in captivity. *Brookesia stumpfii,* a dwarf species from Madagascar, and the African leaf chameleons *(Rhampholeon)* are quite hardy and usually fare better than many other chameleon species. Major breakthroughs have been made in recent years in the care and breeding of chameleons, leading to increasing success with these fascinating lizards.

Basilisks (Genus *Basiliscus*): Basilisks are generally hardy once they are established and a few basic requirements have been provided (such as large enclosures, preferably including plants). The brown basilisk *(Basiliscus basiliscus)* and the spectacular green or double-crested basilisk *(Basiliscus plumifrons)* are now bred in some numbers.

Anoles (Genus *Anolis*): Many species of anoles, including the popular green anole *(Anolis carolinensis)*, fare well in captivity and breed regularly. The green anole and the brown anole *(Anolis sagrei)* are highly recommended for beginners and display well in naturalistic vivaria. The knight anole *(Anolis equestris)*, introduced into Florida from Cuba, is the largest of the genus; it is very adaptable to captivity and is regularly available. This genus has generally been neglected by American herpetoculturists, even though many species make outstanding vivarium display animals.

Curly-tailed lizards (Leiocephalinae): The terrestrial curly-tailed lizards *(Leiocephalus)* are generally hardy and highly recommended as vivarium lizards.

Girdle-tailed lizards and **African plated lizards** (Family Cordylidae): Members of the genera *Cordylus*, *Pseudocordylus* and *Gerrhosaurus* are generally hardy captives, as are some of the larger Madagascar plated lizards *(Zonosaurus)*, such as *Zonosaurus maximus* and *Zonosaurus quadrilineatus*. Some of the *Gerrhosaurus*, such as *Gerrhosaurus major*, become quite tame.

Lacertas (Family Lacertidae): Many of the lacertids adapt very well to captivity, particularly species of *Lacerta and Podarcis*. Several species have been bred in captivity. Beyond making good display animals, many become quite tame.

Skinks (Family Scincidae): Many species of skinks fare well in captivity if provided with the proper type of vivarium. Desert-dwelling burrowers, such as ocellated skinks *(Chalcides ocellatus)* and sandfish *(Scincus scincus)*, should be provided with sand to burrow in. Tropical forest skinks and temperate forest skinks should have a substrate to burrow in, as well as climbing areas of cork bark. Obtaining information on a species' habitat will be important in determining proper vivarium design.

Legless lizards: These are the limbless members of the family Anguidae. The two European species are easily maintained in captivity. One slow worm *(Anguis fragilis)* allegedly lived in captivity to the ripe old age of 54 years. The largest species, the sheltopuzik *(Ophisaurus apodus)* of southeastern Europe and southwestern Asia, is occasionally imported and very hardy. However, these two species should be cooled down in the winter to do well long-term. The United States species are somewhat more difficult to keep in captivity.

Monitor lizards (Family Varanidae): Smaller species of monitors are insectivorous and are occasionally offered by specialized reptile dealers. Australian ridge-tailed monitors *(Varanus acanthurus)* are available on rare occasions as captive-bred specimens. Green tree monitors *(Varanus prasinus)* and Timor monitors *(Varanus timorensis)*, currently imported in small numbers from Indonesia, are primarily insectivorous. Nearly all the larger monitor species start off as insect-eating lizards before graduating to become vertebrate-eating carnivores.

Difficult Species
The following species are difficult to keep alive long-term in captivity and are recommended for specialists only:
    Butterfly agama *(Leiolepis belliana)*
    Toad-headed agamas *(Phrynocephalus)*
    Horned lizards *(Phrynosoma)*
    Australian moloch *(Moloch horridus)*

The following are moderately difficult and are not recommended for beginners:
    Prehensile-tailed iguanids *(Polychrus marmoratus)*
    Casque-headed lizard *(Corythophanes cristatus)*
    Calotes species
    Cnemidophorus species
    Many Chilean species
    True chameleons, except *Bradypodion thamnobates, Chamaeleo calyptratus* and bent-toed geckos *(Cyrtodactylus)*

Size Considerations
Large lizards, such as basilisks, green water dragons, green tree monitors (yes, this is an insect-eating species), bearded

dragons, etc., require relatively large enclosures, along with more extensive lighting and heating than smaller species. Larger animals tend to damage or destroy live plants in a display and may alter the landscape. Also, compared to smaller species, larger species require more frequent maintenance. Large lizards eat larger prey, more food per meal, and consequently defecate greater volumes than smaller species.

If ease of handling is an important consideration, then a medium-to-large species, such as a leopard gecko, lacerta, Sudan plated lizard, or bearded dragon, is usually a better choice than a smaller species.

Miniature Species

Many of the smaller species of lizards have been neglected by herpetoculturists. Unfortunately, humans tend to focus initially on what is most obvious. Something big and colorful and outrageously different draws our attention away from our routine experiential repertoire. If you have never paid attention to reptiles before, big reptiles will shake you out of your unconsciousness and make you notice them. Indeed, large snakes and large lizards are among the best crowd-drawing displays in zoos. People often stand and stare at the animals for awhile, their minds temporarily fascinated and sometimes frightened at the same time.

On the other hand, miniature reptiles require a special kind of attention and often appeal to those who notice the small details in their world. Anyone who has marveled at the degree of miniaturization that can be achieved by nature, at the incredible detail of physical features, subtle color and expression of the smallest forms of life, is in for a treat with miniature lizards (snout-to-vent length usually under 2 1/2 inches). For those who haven't yet taken the time to notice them, spend a few minutes focusing on miniature species. A heretofore unknown aspect of the world may open to you. One aspect of miniature species which has fascinated the author is how animals with such small brains can perform relatively complex behaviors.

For those in the know, the advantages of miniature species are many:

1. They don't require large vivaria.
2. Most miniature lizards are relatively inexpensive.

3. You can keep a variety of miniature species in a relatively small space.

4. Miniature lizards can be kept in naturalistic vivaria because they usually do not damage the landscape.

5. The maintenance of miniature species is less demanding than that of larger species, in part because small lizards have small feces.

6. Many miniature species can be kept in groups. Because of this, a wide variety of behaviors can be observed, including captive breeding.

7. Some species can be mixed in a naturalistic vivarium. This can make for an outstanding display, because you can house a relatively large number of animals if you keep them in a large enclosure.

At one time, the biggest problem with miniature species was finding a source for small insects; but crickets are now available in a variety of sizes and several species of small insects can easily be raised. Among the best species of miniature lizards are the miniature geckos (*Tropiocolotes, Stenodactylus, Gonatodes, Sphaerodactylus, Coleonyx*, some of the dwarf day geckos including *Phelsuma* and *Lygodactylus*, dwarf Australian *Diplodactylus*), the smaller species of lacertids, several species of skinks, Utas and the dwarf chameleons of the genera *Brookesia* and *Rhampholeon*. There are many others, and herpetoculturists interested in these lizards usually watch for new miniature species as they become available.

North American Lizards

These lizards have been generally neglected by United States herpetoculturists. Perhaps they believe: (1) that they are common (and therefore not worth the trouble), or; (2) that non-native species are more challenging and interesting. One of the possible consequences of this short-sighted perspective is that several United States species may one day become unavailable to herpetoculturists. Indeed, there is currently a legislative trend, not always sound in its reasoning and implementation, towards protecting native species and restricting collection of animals from the wild. Many United States species are outstanding and would be greatly missed if they were no longer available to hobbyists. Some of the species which should be established as self-sustaining, captive-propagated populations include the various species and morphs of the collared lizards

(Crotaphytus), banded geckos *(Coleonyx),* various desert spiny lizards *(Sceloporus),* desert iguanas *(Dipsosaurus dorsalis),* chuckwallas *(Sauromalus obesus)* and alligator lizards *(Gerrhonotus).* Collection of these species from the wild should be primarily for the purpose of establishing them in herpetoculture rather than for their wholesale to the pet trade.

In areas where these species occur naturally, the use of outdoor vivaria is the most recommended method for their herpetoculture.

Know your enemies!
Animals rights organizations have dangerous and destructive agendas, including to put an end to animal keeping and human/animal interrelationships. If you support herpetoculture and care about the conservation of biodiversity, do **not** support or join organizations such as PeTA (People for the ethical Treatment of Animals) and the Humane Society of the United States (HSUS). Do **not** confuse animal rights with animal welfare; the terms and the issues are as different as night and day. (see Marquardt, et al., 1993.)

A collared lizard *(Crotaphytus collaris).* When captive-bred and -raised, this United States species is attractive and tends to be very tame. *Crotaphytus* species are quite varied and should be a focus of herpetoculturists. Photo by Alan Anderson.

Selection of Insect-Eating Lizards

One key component of success with insect-eating lizards is to initially select healthy animals. Any altruistic notions of saving that poor, skinny, ill animal in a pet store should be put out of mind immediately. (I know I'm going to get letters about how "If I hadn't decided to buy that poor sick lizard kept in abominable conditions in that horrible store, I never would have experienced the great joy that my little Sherman has brought into my life.") Generally, thin and sick-looking lizards die. If you have never kept lizards before, experiences with sick lizards are likely to discourage you. If you have other lizards, you risk introducing diseases into your collection. Only more experienced keepers with quarantine facilities should ever consider obtaining substandard, less-than-healthy-appearing or thin lizards. Sometimes, because a species is very rare or seldom available, specialists obtain whatever specimens they can in an attempt to establish them in herpetoculture. However, at the outset they are fully aware of the risks involved.

The selection of a lizard (at species and individual levels) can be the most critical factor in determining your success at keeping lizards in captivity.

Selecting a Potentially Healthy Lizard

Now that you have learned this important lesson of choosing the lizard that best meets your needs and desires, the next step is to select a potentially healthy animal to the best of your ability.

The following guidelines should assist you in your selection:

1. Look at a group of lizards or at an individual specimen. Healthy lizards tend to be active with their eyes wide open when moving. Take some time to observe a lizard you are considering buying. Watch the way it moves about the enclosure. Notice if something may be off in its walk. Is it dragging a foot or having trouble keeping its body up off the ground? Does it gape or forcibly exhale air on a regular basis? If so, this

Open-top enclosures for raising large numbers of bearded dragons *(Pogona vitticeps)*. Under most circumstances, screen tops are recommended to prevent escapes and access by children and pets.

Oudoor screen-covered vivaria set up for the commercial breeding of bearded dragons.

may be a sign of respiratory infection. Observe the group. Are there a number of sick-looking animals? If so, be aware that the healthy-appearing lizard(s) you select may have been exposed to some parasites and/or diseases.

2.   Once you have decided on a particular animal, ask that it be handed to you. Many pet store personnel may be reluctant to hand you a lizard. In those cases, simply ask that the animal be presented to you so that you can observe it. A healthy lizard feels like it has a certain amount of weight for its size when held in the hand. Many lizard species demonstrate a definite level of activity when held and give a clear impression of muscular vigor. In a healthy lizard, the tail is rounded or (if it is a species with a flattened tail) an apparent fullness can usually be seen. In any case, the outline of the tail bones should not be visible. A lizard with good weight has a rounded hip area. In underweight lizards the outline of the upper surface of the hip bones and of the backbone becomes apparent, and with very thin lizards the hip bones, backbone and sometimes ribs (e.g., in true chameleons) become very prominent. Avoid thin lizards.

Note: Lizards that are very nervous and frightened, particularly geckos, may drop their tails when handled. You might want to make the best judgment possible without unnecessary handling of these animals.

---

3.   Examine digits and limbs and look for unusual swellings, lumps or missing digits. Check the back and belly for limb or skin damage. Look around the vent. The anal scale(s) should lie flat against the body. There should not be any swelling or crusting or unusual depression or smeared feces in the vent area. Examine the sides and look for collapsed or broken ribs. In some cases, they appear as depressed areas along the side of the animal; in other cases, as rather sharp projections. As a rule, broken ribs give an asymmetrical appearance to the body of a lizard and are usually quite noticeable.

4.   Look at the head. Check that both eyes are kept wide open. Look for opacities (cloudiness) in the eyes. Look at the head and neck area for lumps or swelling.

5.   Using a thumb, gently press up against the throat of the animal.   Bubbly mucus emerging from the nostrils when

performing this procedure is a reliable indication of a respiratory infection. If the lizard opens its mouth, examine the mouth area. It should be clear of bubbly mucus or any lumps, bleeding or caseous (cheesy-looking) matter.

Close-up of a giant leaf-tail gecko *(Uroplatus fimbriatus)*, captive-raised by the author. This species prefers temperatures in the 70's°F (21.1 to 26.1°C) during the day and will tolerate drops into the low 60's F (16.1 to 17.2°) at night. It requires moderate relative humidity, a drip system, and will benefit from BL blacklights. Photo by Alan Anderson.

Sexing

If you have any intentions of breeding lizards or if you want to keep several specimens of the same species together, it is critical that you sex the animals you are purchasing. The following is a brief outline of how to sex lizards. Clearly, this depends upon there being an observable difference between animals. Fortunately, you will find this to be the case with most species offered in the pet trade.

Sexual Dimorphism

In many species there are differences in form, size and/or color that make the sexes easily recognizable. Good examples of obvious sexual dimorphism are basilisk lizards. Adult males have head and/or dorsal crests, making them unmistakable.

The first step when sexing a species is to look for obvious indications of sexual dimorphism. Several examples follow.

The sexes of green or double-crested basilisks (*Basiliscus plumifrons*) are easily determined as adults because they are sexually dimorphic. Males have cranial, dorsal and caudal crests which females lack.

A female green or double-crested basilisk *(Basiliscus plumifrons).*

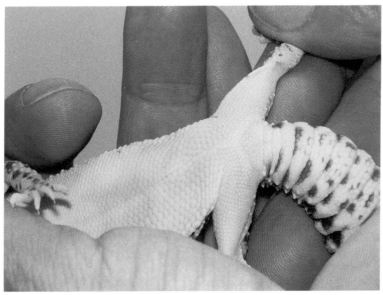

The underside of a female leopard gecko.

1. Differences in:
    a. size, e.g., males are larger than females;
    b. color, e.g., males have orange-red heads;
    c. body proportions, e.g., males have larger heads or females are more heavy bodied;
    d. ornaments and crests, e.g., males have larger crests than females; males have horns;
    e. scalation.

2. Presence of enlarged femoral or preanal pores:
Look at the underside of many lizard species; notice the presence of pores along the underside of the thigh. The pores are often enlarged in males and/or reduced or nearly absent in females. In other species, these enlarged pores are located just anterior to the vent and are called pre-anal pores. In males of the clown agama *(Laudakia stellio brachydactyla)*, there is a midventral line of pores running the length of the belly. These pores secrete waxy scale-like substances (particularly during the breeding season) which are believed to be used in marking territory.

The underside of male leopard gecko. Note the darker pre-anal pores and the pair of bulges at the base of the tail.

The underside of a male four-lined plated lizard from Madagascar (*Zonosaurus quadrilineatus*). Note the femoral pores along the back edge of the thigh.

Clearly visible hemipenile bulge in a male panther chameleon (*Chamaeleo pardalis*).

3. Hemipenile bulges in males
In many species of lizards, clearly defined hemipenile bulges are visible just beyond the vent at the base of the tail. As the term implies, the hemipenile bulge is caused by the inverted hemipenes of males. Looking for hemipenile bulges is a reliable method for sexing many lizards.

Other Methods
Manual eversion of hemipenes
In some species of lizards the differences between males and females may not be obvious. One method of sex determination that is sometimes effective, but which <u>must</u> be performed with extreme care so as to avoid injuring the animal, is to attempt manual eversion of hemipenes. This is done by having one person hold the animal (abdomen facing up) while another -- by applying gentle pressure with the thumb starting at an area at the base of the tail just past where the hemipenes hypothetically end -- rolls the thumb towards the vent to cause eversion of the hemipenes. In lizards, the anal scale(s) often need(s) to be lifted to perform this procedure successfully. This procedure should be learned from an experienced herpetoculturist.

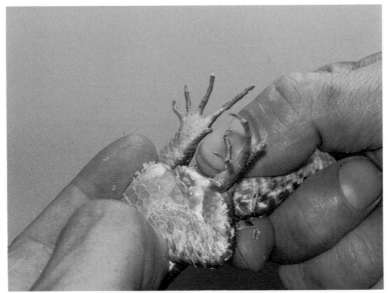

Manual eversion of the hemipenes in a four-lined plated lizard (*Zonosaurus quadrilineatus*). A hemipenis can be seen emerging. This procedure should only be practiced by experienced individuals.

Manual eversion of the hemipenes applied to an inland bearded dragon (*Pogona vitticeps*).

Performed in the wrong manner, it can result in a crushing-type trauma or tail loss. It is effective <u>only</u> with some species, notably certain species of skinks (e.g., *Mabuya* species, *Lygosoma fernandi*) , and is generally ineffective with most species.

Probing

With some species that cannot readily be sexed, sexing probes are sometimes used. This requires experience and involves pulling back the anal scale(s) to better expose the vent. A small probe is inserted <u>very gently</u> into one of the small openings on either side of the vent. In males of some species, because of the presence of inverted hemipenes, the probe penetrates deeper than it does in females. The openings on the sides of the vents of females, when present, are openings to post-anal glands and do not usually allow a probe as deep as those of males. Some males have hemipenile ridges when inverted, which cause hemipenile constrictions that make probing and accurate sex determination difficult. This procedure also needs to be learned from an experienced herpetoculturist. Because most insect-eating lizards are small and can easily be injured with this method, it is <u>not</u> generally recommended.

Behavioral differences

If in doubt about the sex of certain lizards, observing the behavior of animals often offers valuable clues. When in breeding condition, many male lizards perform territorial displays and aggressive, as well as reproductive, behaviors which make their sex unmistakable. Obviously, any lizard that lays eggs and/or gives birth is a female.

Veterinary methods

Specialized veterinarians can perform other sexing methods, such as X-rays, caudal saline injections and laparoscopy, on animals that cannot readily be sexed. Hopefully, the other methods discussed above will allow you to sex most insect-eating lizards without resorting to such procedures.

A *Cordylus* species. As a rule, these lizards are a hardy, adaptable group. Unfortunately, they have a low reproductive rate and thus may one day be no longer available, if their commercial collection is not managed. Efforts should be made to establish a variety of cordylids in herpetoculture. Photo by Alan Anderson.

Quarantine & Acclimation

Note: If you are purchasing a lizard for the first time and/ or do not own animals other than the one you have just obtained, this section may not apply to you. If you think you will be buying other animals in the future, then definitely read this section.

If you have purchased several lizards from the same enclosure in captivity, it is recommended that these lizards be quarantined and kept individually. However, many herpetoculturists keep animals from the same group together and quarantine them that way in order to save on space and labor.

After careful selection, quarantine and acclimation are two important steps in the successful keeping of insect-eating lizards. It is important for any herpetoculturist to realize that if a lizard is not captive-bred and -raised (which applies to only a minority of those sold in the trade), it will have been wild-collected. It will also be infested with a number of parasites and is likely to have been exposed to a number of disease-causing organisms. Stressful conditions are common during an animal's initial period in captivity; parasites can increase to life-threatening levels and the lizard may very well become much more susceptible to disease. It is critical that a herpetoculturist <u>never introduce a wild-caught lizard into an established collection without first quarantining the animals</u>.

For most species this means keeping a new lizard by itself in a quarantine enclosure isolated from any other lizards in one's collection, preferably in a separate room. The quarantine enclosure should be simply designed, yet should also provide the basic requirements of the animal, including a suitable substrate, basking areas and shelters, heat, and light. (With all <u>but</u> fossorial species, newsprint is recommended as substrate during quarantine.) The minimum recommended quarantine period is 30 days, with 60 to 90 days being preferred. The quarantine period should be a time of special attention. During this period you should daily spend varying amounts of time observing the animal and adjusting your maintenance schedules and procedures to meet its needs.

The quarantine procedure will enable you to determine the following:

1. Whether an animal is feeding and drinking and whether it is maintaining or gaining weight. It will also allow you to determine food preferences. For example, some of the small ant-eating agamas will feed on medium crickets in captivity but they will invariably regurgitate them. If offered smaller crickets and fruit flies, the lizards will keep them down and gain weight.

2. The status of an animal's stools. Because of poor diet and other factors (including stress), it is common for newly imported animals to have soft stools. After a few days to a week, most animals should defecate the formed stools characteristic of a healthy lizard. Animals with persistently runny or discolored stools often have a gastroenteric disease that needs to be diagnosed and treated. The use of newsprint as a substrate allows you to easily assess the status of the stools.

The initial stages of quarantine of a group of frog-eyed geckos. Note the regurgitated mealworm masses near the water dish. Note runny stool mass and the large "water ring" on right. Following treatment with Flagyl® (metronidazole), this group established and bred.

3. **The presence of parasites.** External parasites (ticks and mites) can be observed and treated. Internal parasites are best determined by a fecal exam but many herpetoculturists, particularly with smaller and inexpensive species, routinely treat their animals with Panacur® (fenbendazole) at a dosage of 50 mg/kg (an accurate scale is required) for nematodes, and Flagyl® (metronidazole) at a dosage of 75 mg/kg for protozoans. The treatment is repeated in 10 to 15 days. Some type of training is recommended before attempting home parasite treatment because of the risk of overdosage if one does not calculate accurately. (Two recommended references are Klingenberg 1993 and Frye 1991.) Another approach which is, in fact, used by most lizard keepers is to simply observe the animal. If it is feeding, maintaining good weight, and has healthy-appearing stools, it is presumed to be free of life-threatening levels of parasites.

4. **Whether an animal is sick.** Indications of illness are failure to feed, listlessness, weight loss, runny and/or discolored stools, swellings of limbs or lumps on the body, inability to

Healthy stools will be formed and often accompanied by white urates. The "water ring" around a stool can also be used as a measure of health. Typically, runny or watery stools will have "water rings" more than twice the diameter of the stool mass.

move or to keep eyes open, sunken eyes, unusual behaviors (such as twitching of hind legs) or spasmic behaviors, gaping and forced exhalation (almost always indicates respiratory infection or, on rare occasions, parasites). The sooner you determine a lizard to be ill and the sooner you attempt to determine what is wrong, the better the chances are that it eventually pulls through.

5. Necessary modifications in the vivarium design. A newly purchased lizard in a quarantine situation may be observed to consistently lie rather quietly at the end of the vivarium farthest from the heat source. In this case, the vivarium may be too warm and an alternate thermal gradient may need to be established. In another situation, an animal may always lie beneath or on a heat source, suggesting that the vivarium may not be warm enough. Another lizard may be persistently digging or climbing at walls. All of these behaviors suggest a need for changes in vivarium design.

6. Whether an animal is acclimating to captive conditions. Because of disease and environmental stress, the health of many imported lizards declines. This may sometimes begin subtly, as with gradual weight loss, but it can also take place quite suddenly, even overnight. The sooner you notice a decline and try to discover the cause, the better the chances of the animal turning around. The lizard that acclimates will ultimately have the appearance of improved health, including weight gain, by the time the quarantine period is over.

Some Useful
HerpetoculturalTerms

Herpetoculturists commonly use certain terms to describe the habits or requirements of various lizard species. The following are terms commonly used to describe the behaviors of lizards.

Diurnal: Active during the daytime.

Nocturnal: Active at night.

Crepuscular: Active at dawn or twilight.

Terrestrial: Living or active on the ground surface, e.g., leopard geckos *(Eublepharis macularius)* or curly-tailed lizards *(Leiocephalus)* .

Arboreal: Living or active on trees and shrubs, e.g., knight anoles *(Anolis equestris)* and true chameleons *(Chamaeleo)* .

Semi-arboreal: Living or active on trees and shrubs part of the time, e.g., bearded dragons *(Pogona vitticeps)* and green water dragons *(Physignathus cocincinus)*.

Saxicolous: Living or active among rocks, e.g., Baja blue rock lizard *(Petrosaurus thalassinus)* and cordylids.

Fossorial: Living or active at least part of the time in a substrate such as soil or sand, e.g., sand fish *(Scincus scincus)* and ocellated skinks *(Chalcides ocellatus)*.

Semi-aquatic: Living or active part of the time in water, e.g., crocodile lizards *(Shinisaurus crocodilurus)* and Asian water skinks *(Tropidophorus)*.

Herpetoculturists also use the following terms to arbitrarily group lizards according to climatic/vivarium requirements.

Temperate: Inhabiting either the North Temperate Zone between the Arctic Circle and the Tropic of Cancer or the South Temperate Zone between the Antarctic Circle and the Tropic of Capricorn. In terms of herpetoculture, this refers to lizards exposed to seasonal variations in temperature, including warm summers and cool-to-cold winters. Hibernation (brumation) is generally recommended for these species to breed and to fare well long-term in captivity. Temperate lizards are also subject to annual variations in day length, with long days in the summer and short days in the winter.

Subtropical: Inhabiting areas adjacent to the tropics. In terms of herpetoculture this means lizard species which require warmth during most of the year; they should be exposed to moderately warm daytime temperatures, cooler nights and a reduced photoperiod in the winter. The importance of obtaining species-specific information is addressed below.

Tropical: Inhabiting the tropics. Anyone who has been to the tropics knows that there are many life zones in the tropics and that no generalization can be made on lizard species from tropical areas. Thus, it is critical that one obtain additional information on tropical species. If a lizard is a montane species, it may be subject to slightly warm daytime temperatures and cool, possibly cold, nights. At one time, lack of information regarding the life zones of several species of montane chameleons (including the popular Jackson's chameleon) led to poor husbandry methods which resulted in their being difficult to keep in captivity.

Herpetoculturists normally use the term tropical when referring to species from lowland tropical areas, usually moist tropical forest species rather than dry tropical forest species. The latter usually fare well in desert vivaria; the former in tropical forest floor or tropical forest vivaria. Species from lowland tropical forests typically require warm daytime temperatures in the mid to high 80's°F (26.7 to 31.7°C) and mild nighttime temperatures in the high 70's to low 80's°F (25 to 28.3°C). Relative humidity tends to be high in lowland tropical forest habitats.

Montane: Inhabiting mountain or high-altitude areas. Herpetoculturists, by adding the term montane to the descriptive terms above, intend to indicate that because the species live at a high altitude it has special temperature requirements; either cooler nights or generally cooler temperatures. This usually implies that species will not fare well long-term under a standard warm temperature regimen.

Types of Vivaria

From the point of view of lizard keeping, four types of vivaria are usually considered by lizard keepers: desert, forest floor, tropical forest and shoreline. This is an arbitrary grouping by herpetoculturists that does not necessarily correspond to the established use of the terms or to biomes/life zones (e.g., a desert vivarium is not exclusively for desert-dwelling lizards).

Desert vivarium

This type of vivarium is characterized by a dry substrate, either sand or a fine gravel. It also has one or more hot basking areas created by spotlights, plus one or more shelters. A hot-rock-type heater can be used as a secondary heating source. Rocks and dry woods are used to landscape. Some live plants can also be incorporated, such as sansevierias, ponytail palms, haworthias and others (see Plants). Daytime temperatures should be in the low to mid 80's°F (28.9 to 30°C), with basking areas from 87 to 100°F (30.6 to 37.8°C). This type of vivarium also includes a marked drop in nighttime temperatures, usually down to room temperature (70's°F (21 to 26°C)) during the warm months. Lizards from dry montane areas typically require a greater drop in nighttime temperatures. Relative humidity is typically low to moderate because of the low moisture content of the substrate and high evaporative rate generated by spotlights in desert vivaria. Winter temperatures should be determined by the requirements of the particular species. Water is provided only in a shallow dish. Plants are watered individually at the base.

Lizards recommended for desert vivaria: Desert agamines, including several *Agama* species, bearded dragons *(Pogona)*, many skinks, such as Schneider's skinks, barrel skinks *(Chalcides)*, plated lizards, girdle-tailed lizards (armadillo lizards of the pet trade), lacertids, and geckos from dry/desert/semi-arid areas. With fine sand, this type of vivarium is used with desert/semi-arid region fossorial species, such as sandfish and ocellated skinks. With a moderate relative humitidy, desert vivaria can be used with many tropical dry forest species.

Forest floor/moist substrate vivarium

This type of vivarium should have a barely moist substrate, usually a flaky airy moist potting soil mix or a damp mulch, such as cypress mulch. Some herpetoculturists use seedling orchid bark. The substrate should have sufficient depth for the upper surface to be dry. Depending upon the species one is keeping, attention must be given to the type of substrate used; for some species it needs to be sandier than for certain others, for whom sand may be abrasive. A few rocks or a dried tree stump or root base can be used for landscaping, as can several species of live plants. Several shelters should be included. Relative humidity builds up within the shelters as a result of trapping water evaporation from the substrate. For tropical species a subtank heater is used to maintain an even ground temperature. For montane or temperate species, no subtank heat is required. A spotlight is placed over a basking area (rock or tree stump) so that temperatures are in the mid 80's°F (28.9 to 30°C).

Lizards recommended for forest floor/moist substrate vivaria: Burrowing forest skinks such as several of the small Asian *Mabuya, Lygosoma,* various anguids, such as the European slow worm *(Anguis fragilis)* and some of the galliwasps.

Tropical forest/arboreal lizard vivarium

This type of vivarium is characterized by a dry substrate surface, typically orchid bark or a moist soil mix with a dry upper surface. A basking light is placed over a dried tree stump or (in most cases) over a diagonally placed branch, because many tropical forest lizards are arboreal or semi-arboreal. A sub-tank heater, such as FlexWatt®, should be used to help maintain the vivarium at an evenly warm temperature around the mid 80's°F (28.9 to 30°C) during the day with a 5-10°F (2.8 to 5.5°C) drop at night. A basking light should be placed over a diagonally placed branch or tree stump so that the temperature in the basking section closest to the light is 90-95°F (32.2 to 35°C). Dried woods and live plants can be used for landscaping. Good plants are pothos, Chinese evergreen, dracaenas, *Sansevieria trifasciata* and hybrids, bromeliads such as nerogelias and earth stars *(Cryptanthus),* and many others (see Plants). Relative humidity should be moderate to high, depending upon substrate moisture, plants and misting regimens. Watering for arboreal species is provided primarily by misting but it is a good idea to also place a small shallow water container in the enclosure.

Lizards recommended for tropical forest vivaria: Arboreal lizards including chameleons, anoles, basilisks, arboreal agamines, water dragons, day geckos and many other climbing geckos.

Note: Some herpetoculturists combine in one enclosure features of a forest floor vivarium and a tropical forest vivarium so that they can keep a variety of species together. Large vivaria are required in order to accomplish this.

Shoreline vivarium

This is a vivarium which combines land and water. Because the only semi-aquatic lizard species available in the pet trade at the present time are the water skinks *(Tropidophorus)*, the basic design is simple. In a vivarium at least 24 in. (60.9 cm) long, aquarium gravel is placed in such a manner as to create a ground level sloping into a water section. Rocks are placed at the edge of the water. Freshwater driftwood can also be added to the vivarium. Plants such as pothos, arrowheads *(Syngonium)* and Chinese evergreen *(Aglaonema)* are grown hydroponically. A sub-tank heater on a thermostat can be used to maintain the overall tank temperature in the high 70's°F (25 to 26°C). A basking light is placed over the rocks so that temperature is around the mid 80's°F (28.9 to 30°C) (use a small spotlight). The vivarium can be flushed by pouring water through the gravel and siphoning out through the water section.

Note: In a well-designed vivarium, water skinks make an attractive and interesting display. They will breed in captivity; they give birth to live young.

Other species: Crocodile lizards *(Shinisaurus crocodilurus)* can be kept in the same manner.

Note: Temperatures, substrates and plant selections in the above-described vivarium types can also be adjusted to meet the requirements of various temperate and montane lizard sepcies

---

Housing

Enclosures
All-glass vivaria with screen tops
The author's preferred vivaria are the sliding-glass-front enclosures manufactured by Third Wave Vivaria, Inc., in Boca Raton, Florida. There are also several commercial all-glass enclosures available with sliding screen tops. All-glass enclosures prove useful for keeping and displaying many kinds of insect-eating lizards. Aquarium tanks can also be used, as long as secure-fitting screen tops are constructed and added to the enclosures. For geckos that climb on glass, enclosures with side openings, which are available by special order, are recommended to prevent sudden escapes through the top.

Custom-built enclosures
If you live in an area with a local all-glass vivarium manufacturer, you may also want to consider having vivaria custom built. All-glass vivaria sold commercially do not usually have

A sliding screen-top vivarium by Stay In Reptile®. This type of enclosure is among the least expensive on the market and is suitable for keeping a wide range of reptiles. The sliding screen top can present challenges in terms of enclosure placement, accessing the inside of the enclosure for maintenance and animal escapes (e.g., climbing geckos).

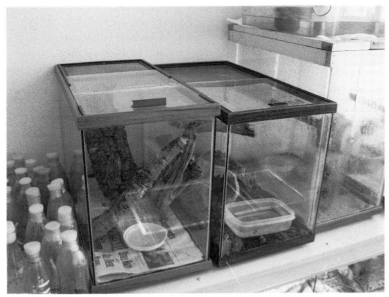

A half glass-, half screen-top enclosure. Heat dispersal is affected by the glass section. The use of a spotlight in smaller enclosures can result in a fatal heat buildup. Larger enclosures of this type present fewer of these problems. This type of enclosure is recommended for animals that require higher relative humidity. There are considerable limitations in terms of heating and lighting. Enclosures with ventilated glass tops have serious limitations in terms of heating and lighting and are not recommended by the author.

sufficient room for interesting stratification (except for the Third Wave Vivaria enclosures mentioned earlier). Placing a background of rock or cork bark in these tanks usually takes up so much of the available width and/or depth that it significantly restricts the amount of remaining open space.

Larger enclosures can be constructed using wood bottoms and sides, glass fronts, and screened covers. If wood is used, several coats of marine epoxy paint or clear polyurethane will seal the wood against moisture (be sure the product you choose is safe for the animals). Custom-made enclosures constructed of wood or melamine with sliding glass doors in front are now available from individuals and small companies specializing in reptile enclosures (e.g., Sandmar, El Cajon, California). These are suitable only for animals that can be kept on a dry substrate. Very large custom enclosures can be built using aluminum-frame windows or fiberglass tub enclosures or shower stalls with clear glass doors.

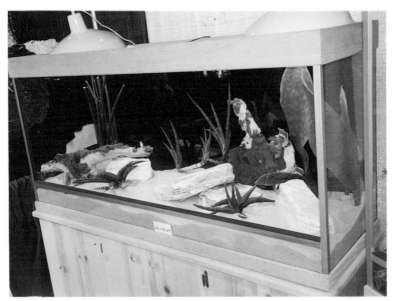

A sliding-glass front vivarium. This type is ideal for those interested in naturalistic vivarium design. With front opening vivaria, some care needs to be given when accessing the front in order to prevent the escape of animals (although they usually move away from you, toward the back) and food insects. In terms of ease of access, ease of maintenance and aesthetics, this is the author's first choice for lizard vivaria.

A naturalistic vivarium designed for keeping small day geckos. Snake plants, pothos, Cape honeysuckle and an epiphytic cactus are growing in this vivarium.

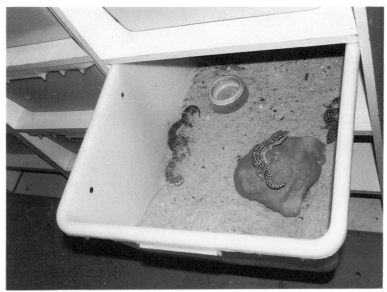

Some commercial breeders of leopard geckos use storage box/shelf systems for housing breeding groups and hatchlings. Care must be given to provide ventilation by perforating the sides of boxes with either a drill (which can crack hard plastics) or a soldering iron (use only in a well-ventilated area).

Lizards should <u>not</u> be kept in cramped small plastic boxes. Think quality of life when keeping animals. Illustration by Kevin Anderson.

A section of the shelf system is heated by a recessed heat cable on a rheostat or thermostat. With additional modifications (alternating shelves and cutting out and screening in part of an upper shelf), fluorescent lighting can be added to these systems. However, they are only recommended for small-to-medium terrestrial lizards, particularly geckos.

Do not use acrylic aquarium tanks or plexiglass-sided enclosures to house lizards. The animals scratch the sides to the point that the aesthetic appeal of the enclosure is eventually lost.

Open-top vivaria

With terrestrial lizards, particularly species from desert or semi-arid habitats, open-top vivaria can be used. Custom-made enclosures made of wood, melamine, preformed large plastic tubs or troughs, and fiberglass enclosures, including small hot tubs, are suitable for this type of setup. Creating a lip around the inside of the upper edge minimizes the risk of escape. To assure that an animal which might accidentally escape remains within a limited area, these vivaria should be kept in a room with a door that closes securely, leaving little space under the door. Any small holes in walls, etc., should be sealed.

Interesting naturalistic landscapes can be designed with open-top vivaria if the bottom is made waterproof with a custom plexiglass liner (inserted in the bottom of the enclosure), a polyethylene liner (sold in rolls in hardware stores), or a pool liner (obtainable from stores or nurseries offering materials for water gardens). This type of vivarium is not recommended if one has cats, dogs or unpredictable children. Consideration might be given to keeping such vivaria in locked rooms.

Never use open-top vivaria outdoors without adding a tight-fitting screen cover.

Wire-mesh- and screen-sided vivaria

Plastic-coated, welded wire mesh cages and aviaries are suitable for large chameleons and some large arboreal lizards (plain wire mesh is <u>not</u> appropriate). Screen-sided vivaria made of aluminum or plastic screen are suitable for keeping chameleons, anoles and small lizards, as long as attention is given to providing proper relative humidity. However, these vivaria are seldom visually attractive, having considerable limitations in terms of design and landscaping potential.

Plastic storage boxes

For large-scale maintenance of nocturnal terrestrial geckos, polyethylene and polystyrene (e.g., Rubbermaid®) plastic storage boxes, with small perforations placed in the top and sides

Screen-sided cages, which allow for plenty of ventilation, are a good way to allow lizards to bask in sunlight. <u>Always</u> make shelter or shade available to help avoid the potential for overheating your animals.

for air flow, have proven to be economical and space-saving enclosures. They can be kept on shelves heated with recessed heat tape or narrow FlexWatt® heat strips which run the length of the shelf underneath the boxes and are controlled by thermostat or rheostat. For large-scale maintenance of small diurnal lizards, plastic storage boxes can be used if a custom screen cover is built and a light source is placed above. Several gecko breeders prefer a screen top with light over a perforated top.

Plastic terraria

Commercially sold plastic terraria are not generally recommended for keeping insect-eating lizards. They can prove useful for some very small species of lizards, but for the most part their use is limited. Most plastic terraria are too small and the plastic can melt when exposed to heat sources. The plastic also eventually becomes scratched, resulting in poor visibility. However, they are useful for raising and segregating baby lizards if they are kept in heated rooms and only fluorescent full-spectrum lighting is used as a heat source. Breeders of geckos and true chameleons find them very useful during the early stages of rearing these lizards.

These containers are also practical for transporting smaller lizards and are very useful for housing insects to be gut-loaded.

Outdoor vivaria

In areas where the climate is moderate, insect-eating lizards can be kept in outdoor vivaria for part of the year or year round. Specially designed greenhouses, screen houses or custom-built outdoor vivaria are suitable for this purpose. Careful thought needs to be given to the design of these outdoor vivaria; attention should be given to providing the same general conditions as in indoor vivaria, although the means may vary. For example, the sun can provide light and heat, while water can be supplied through automated misters or drip systems. During the winter months heat must be provided through a heating system or the animals will need to be brought indoors. It is not within the scope of this book to provide details on the design of outdoor vivaria. This will be covered by the author in a future work.

Size of Enclosures

In terms of enclosure size, generally a vivarium should have a length at least four times the total length of the largest lizard

One of the most common mistakes is buying enclosures that are too small to accommodate growing lizards.

and a width at least one and a half times the length of the largest lizard. For naturalistic vivaria containing plants and elaborate landscaping, the vivarium should be at least five times the length of the largest lizard. The author prefers larger vivaria, at least eight times the length of the largest lizard for small species and at least four times the length of the largest lizard for medium to large species. Obviously, taller vivaria are recommended for use with arboreal or semi-arboreal species. It is important to think in terms of "quality of life" when keeping reptiles, just as one would with other kinds of animals.

Density of Animals

Reptiles fare best when they are not overcrowded. The author recommends low densities of animals with the sum of their total lengths less than three quarters the length (longest dimension) of the enclosure. As a general guideline, if you are mixing two species of lizards which inhabit different niches, such as small lacertas (e.g., *Podarcis muralis*), which are ground- and rock-dwelling, with crocodile geckos *(Tarentola mauritanica)*, which are rock- and bark-climbing (also side-dwellers in vivaria), then the density can be somewhat increased. Remember: The lower the density, the less maintenance required, the lower the stress level and the lower the risk of spreading disease. Often the best basis for deciding animal density is the same as the criteria for effective breeding groups; usually single pairs or trios (one male with two females) of a given species.

On Mixing Species

As a rule, it is best to not mix lizard species, particularly if one is interested in captive breeding. This rule should be followed by anyone who is working with rare species or is serious about captive breeding. However, many herpetoculturists have had good results mixing species, as long as they do not compete for the same vivarium niche. Thus, some people successfully keep together several species of Egyptian lizards, including fossorial species such as ocellated skinks *(Chalcides ocellatus)*, diurnal ground-dwelling species such as lacertas, and rock- or wall-dwelling species such as fan-footed geckos *(Ptyodactylus hasselquisti)* or Moorish geckos *(Tarentola mauritanica)*. Here again, experimentation is required.

A female Natal midland dwarf chameleon *(Bradypodion thamnobates)*. This is one of the hardiest species of chameleons. It should become available in increasing numbers. Photo by Alan Anderson.

Vivarium Design

Steps to Vivarium Design

Once you have information on the species you want to keep and its requirements, you can proceed with the vivarium design and assembly. The following are steps required to assemble a vivarium.

1. Select an enclosure.
2. Place enclosure on a stand or select an item of furniture to serve as a stand.
3. If a subtank heating system is used, place the heater under the enclosure.
4. Place the substrate(s) in the bottom of the enclosure.
5. Add landscape structures, including shelters, basking areas, rocks and wood.
6. Add plants and possibly add more surface layer substrate.
7. Place the cover over the top.
8. Add lights and other heating systems.
9. Add monitoring equipment such as timers, thermometers, hygrometers.

A vivarium (4 ft. in length) by Third Wave Vivaria, Inc., designed for combining small-to-medium-size arboreal and terrestrial lizards.

10. Make adjustments as required.

The next chapter introduces you to supplies and elements available for the creation of vivaria for insect-eating lizards.

> **Ants** can be the nemesis of lizard keepers. These insects can be unintentionally introduced into a vivarium with live plants. They can trail and swarm to feed on dead food insects and fruit nectars. They may try to set up a colony within the vivarium. Sometimes they will swarm and kill baby lizards. **Inspect plants very carefully before introducing them into a vivarium**. Also, be sure to control ant populations. With some lizard species, such as day geckos and true chameleons, babies may have to be raised in watertight enclosures sitting in shallow containers of water. Some chameleon keepers put the legs of custom-built enclosure stands in containers filled with motor oil or water to keep out ants. **Beware**: It is **much** easier to guard against ants beforehand than it is to deal with them after you have established a vivarium.

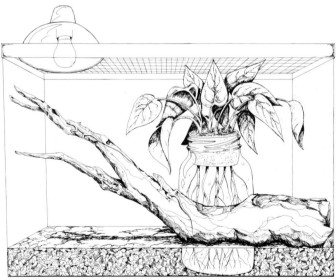

A basic tropical vivarium for green anoles, day geckos and other small tropical lizards. A spotlight provides heat. Pothos or Chinese evergreen can be grown hydroponically in a jar of water. Orchid bark is used as a substrate. In cool areas, additional heating, in the form of a heat strip, may be necessary. Illustration by Glen Warren.

Substrates

For many species of desert lizards, various sands, gravels and sand/soil mixes make suitable substrates. For desert species that dig burrows, use a substrate consisting of 50% sand and 50% potting soil, or a sandy soil containing clay, at one end of the enclosure. Moisten that section and then pat down the soil to compress it. The rest of the vivarium can contain sand. When it dries, the compressed soil usually retains the necessary cohesion to allow for digging a burrow. If you live near a desert, consider using natural desert soils. Some vivarists search for the larger-grained sand and soils found at the entrances of nests of certain large ants. When available, decomposed granite sands are excellent for desert vivaria.

> **Note: Fine silica sand is not recommended for active digging species because of a possible risk of silicosis of the lungs. Also, silica sand may abrade and scar the GI tract of baby lizards if it is ingested.**

For forest species and arboreal species, many herpetoculturists use a fine-to-medium grade orchid bark (use a grade large enough so that it cannot be readily swallowed), which is attractive and retains some moisture when dampened. A good quality moistened potting soil (without perlite) can also be used effectively with these species. The surface of potting soil should be allowed to dry, or a thin layer of dry substrate, such as orchid bark, should be added. In designing naturalistic vivaria for use with small forest or arboreal species, a substrate consisting of a peat-base potting soil with 10 to 20% medium-grade sand and 10 to 20% fine orchid bark to increase drainage works well if the mixture is placed over a 1 1/2 in.(3.8 cm) layer of pebbles which serves as a drainage layer. An orchid bark substrate presents problems with small species because food items (small crickets) are able to hide all too easily.

Landscaping

How one landscapes a vivarium depends upon the needs and behaviors of its inhabitants. Arboreal and climbing lizards should be provided with dried branches, sections of wood or cork bark slabs for climbing. Rock-climbing species from desert areas should have vertical sections of cholla wood, dried wood sections, or cork bark. Rock-climbing areas can also be constructed using rocks, but <u>great</u> care should be taken to assure that the rocks cannot shift or fall, accidentally crushing the lizards. Silicone cement will hold rocks together and help to prevent these mishaps. Hot glue also works with some kinds of rock. Generally, lighter substitutes, such as sand-blasted woods, cholla skeleton, and cork make maintenance easier (you won't ever have to lift heavy rocks) and are safer for the animals. There are now plastic landscape materials simulating rocks and/or wood that are also suitable. Fiberglass backgrounds copied directly from rocky areas are an alternative which will be available in the near future.

Cork bark, which is available as cork rounds (hollow logs) and flat cork, is one of the most useful and versatile of vivarium landscape materials.

An imported leaf-tail gecko with a shedding problem. Without the appropriate relative humidity or humidified shelters, many lizards will have problems shedding; the dry shed skin will remain adhered to the body. Photo by Nola Anderson.

Shelters

Except for arboreal species that sleep on branches, <u>all</u> lizards should be provided with some kind of shelter.

Vertical shelters

Climbing lizards, such as geckos, require vertical shelters which are easily created with vertically placed slabs of cork bark or rock leaning against the side of the enclosure. Take care to anchor rocks well to prevent crushing.

Horizontal shelters

Terrestrial lizards require horizontal shelters. These are shelters that are placed over the substrate of the vivarium. There are several attractive, commercially-produced shelters of formed concrete, plastic, ceramic, or clay that work well. Cork bark is another excellent choice for horizontal shelters. Shelters can also be made from broken sections of clay pots or by resting one thin rock over another. When using rocks, care must be given to not accidentally crush lizards when removing or moving rocks. Silicone sealant or hot glue can hold rocks together and help to reduce that risk.

This vivarium includes examples of vertical (left) and horizontal (ground level) shelters. The basking lizard is a captive-born Indonesian blue-tongue skink *(Tiligua gigas)*.

Above-ground shelters

Some arboreal lizards, such as prehensile-tail geckos *(Rhacodactylus)* and a number of rock-dwelling lizards, prefer above-ground shelters. To create these, shelter areas should be placed on a horizontal platform or shelf. These platforms can be created by siliconing glass sections to the walls of the enclosure. Other methods are to silicone pieces of cork bark or wood together and/or to the sides of the vivarium. Rock can also be siliconed to the walls of the vivarium for this purpose, but beware of the risk of lizards being crushed and of glass breaking. As should be obvious, access to these above-ground shelters should be created using sections of cork, wood or rock.

Humidified shelters

One of the features of shelters and burrows in the wild, particularly in drier habitats, is that the relative humidity inside a shelter is significantly higher than in the open air. The result is that reptiles in shelters lose less water while breathing. The higher relative humidity also facilitates shedding. Humidified shelters have been used with a variety of reptiles. They have proven particularly useful with certain desert geckos, such as frog-eyed geckos *(Teratoscincus)*, fat-tail geckos *(Hemitheconyx caudicinctus)* and the Australian eyelash geckos *(Diplodactylus)*. When acclimating certain species, these shelters aid in reducing life-threatening water loss.

The following are three approaches to creating humidified shelters:

1. One method employed by many gecko keepers is the use of an oversize shelter with a small shallow dish of sand and/or pebbles placed in the center. The substrate-filled dish is then sprayed regularly so that the contents stay moist. Lizards can choose the dry or the moist substrate as they prefer.

2. Soaked clay shelters: Shelters of red kiln-baked clay have water-holding qualities that contribute to relative humidity. Simply place the shelter in water for about an hour; then use it as a shelter. As the water evaporates, humidity is increased. This soaking procedure needs to be repeated every one to three days.

3. Placing a small non-tippable water container in the shelter. For example, a small container, such as an empty film canister, can be attached to the side of a shelter using silicone sealer. The canister can then be filled with water. As the water evaporates it raises the relative humidity.

Basking Areas

Most diurnal lizards require a basking area, over which a high temperature is generated, in order to fare well. This helps to establish a gradient whereby the temperature diminishes with distance from the heat source. For terrestrial lizards, a standard procedure for creating a basking area is to place an incandescent light (either a regular household lightbulb or a spotlight) in a reflector-type fixture above the screen top of a vivarium so that heat is radiated onto a flat rock. For arboreal lizards, branches or interesting sections of wood or tree root are placed diagonally along the length of the vivarium as climbing areas. An incandescent light is placed above the screen of the vivarium so that heat is radiated from the upper to the middle portion of the angled wood section, allowing lizards to thermoregulate depending upon the distance they choose from the heat source. When keeping several lizards together, two or more basking sites should be provided. Dominant animals may bully submissive individuals away from the site if there is only one.

Hot-rock-type heaters and reptile heating pads are useful with some terrestrial and nocturnal species, but with most diurnal terrestrial species they are recommended only as secondary heat sources. Many lizards associate basking with light. <u>Hot rocks should not be used as a substitute for meeting the lighting requirements of lizards.</u>

Careful attention should be given to properly closing screen covers or sliding glass fronts to prevent animals from escaping. Illustration by Kevin Anderson.

Naturalistic Vivarium Design

This term refers to vivarium design whereby some of the essential elements of an animal's habitat are simulated by using live plants and a variety of landscape materials. One key to this approach is that an actual reproduction of the animal's natural habitat is not usually attempted because the native plants and landscape materials are rarely available. Also, plants from the natural habitat seldom fare well over time inside a vivarium. Thus, vivarists select plants which are known to grow well in vivaria. As landscape materials, one may also choose cork bark, lightweight fiberglass reproductions of rock or wood, or rocks made of formed concrete in place of natural rock. Artistic latitude is one of the privileges afforded in naturalistic vivarium design. The goal is to create an environment which allows the animals maintained to fare well and display a wide range of behaviors; also one that is aesthetically appealing and will hold its own as a display, even with no animals present. One important factor in successful vivarium design is low animal density; this minimizes maintenance and damage to the display. Naturalistic vivarium design is part of mainstream European herpetoculture.

Plants
Plants add considerable appeal to a vivarium housing insect-eating lizards. Many herpetoculturists place plants in pots and bury the pots in the substrate or conceal them with landscape structures. Some place plants directly in the ground medium when keeping small lizards in naturalistic vivaria. Certain plants can be placed in jars of water and grown hydroponically. The selection of plants for vivaria requires special consideration. Amphibians and reptiles are active animals, capable of crushing, tearing and uprooting many commonly sold houseplants and terrarium plants. The author has experimented with a wide range of plants in vivarium design and has created many successful naturalistic vivaria. (*The Vivarium Handbook, Part 1, Desert and Tropical Vivarium Design* is scheduled to be published by Advanced Vivarium Systems in 1994.)

Sources of plants
Plants suitable for vivaria can be found in supermarkets, department stores, plant shops and nurseries. For those who

live in isolated areas or who want unusual species not normally sold in stores, the best way to obtain interesting vivarium plants is through mail-order. Check house plant publications for sources.

Vivarium plants

It is not within the scope of this book to list all plant species suitable for vivaria. The following plant species are relatively easy to obtain and fare well under the conditions indicated:

For desert vivaria

Haworthias
Gasteraloes
Oxtongue or bowtie plants *(Gasteria)*
Gasterhaworthia "Royal Highness"
Ponytail palms *(Beaucarnea recurvata)*
Snake plants *(Sansevieria)*, some of the best vivarium plants
Lace Aloe *(Aloe aristata)*
Partridge breast aloe *(Aloe variegata)*
Climbing aloe *(Aloe ciliaris)*
Geranium species *(Pelargonium)*
Caudexed figs *(Ficus palmeri* and *Ficus petiolaris)*

A desert vivarium (2 ft x 2 ft x 2 ft) designed by the author for housing one pair of collared lizards *(Crotaphytus collaris)* and one pair of Jones' armadillo lizards *(Cordylus jonesi).*

Note: Some cacti with no spines or with harmlessly recurved spines can be tried, but the risk of etiolation (lack of sun and/ or enough light, resulting in deformed and elongated growth) is high. For this reason, the author has not listed cacti here.

For tropical vivaria

Pothos *(Epipremnum aureum)*

Chinese evergreen *(Aglaonema)*

Snake plants *(Sansevieria)*, many species and quite variable

Bromeliads *(Neoregelia, Billbergia, Guzmania, Aechmea)*, spiny edges can present problems with large lizard species

Earth stars *(Cryptanthus)*

Rosary vine *(Ceropegia woodii)*

Weeping fig *(Ficus benjamina)*

Various Gesneriads, particularly *Nematanthus* and *Aeschynanthus*

Dwarf scheffelera *(Brassaia actinophylla)*

Dracaenas (in small sizes; they eventually outgrow a vivarium)

Creeping fig *(Ficus pumila)*

Orchids *(Dendrobium, Epidendrum, Haemaria, Oncidium* and many others)

A vivarium designed by the author for housing one male and three female frog-eyed geckos *(Teratoscincus keyzerlingii)*.

The interest in naturalistic vivarium design is just beginning to catch on among United States herpetoculturists. This is probably the most exciting and promising area in the future of herpetoculture.

A closeup of a section of a large tropical vivarium designed by the author. This particular vivarium allows for tree frogs, poison-dart frogs, anoles and small day geckos to be kept together.

Temperature

There are currently several books on the market, some species-specific, that provide information on the temperature requirements of various lizards. Unfortunately, many of the lizard species sold in the trade are not covered in these books; also, some of the temperature ranges suggested by the authors are wrong. In many cases you will have to find a temperature range that works based on your personal observations of a lizard's behavior in captivity. The first step is to obtain the name of the species you are planning to purchase and to look for information on the country of origin, and habitat, if possible. Remember: most countries have varied landscapes with many different temperature ranges. An animal living in a tropical country is actually exposed to cool temperatures if it comes from high altitude montane areas. High altitude habitats are also subject to greater day/night fluctuations in temperature than lower elevation habitats. For example, numerous lizards that were once imported by the tens of thousands from Chile were actually high altitude lizards which probably required significant day/night temperature variations in order to fare well. Many of these lizards died within a few months in captivity. Animals that live near the ground of primary tropical forest or under the canopy of tropical forest are exposed to significantly cooler temperatures than those living along the edges of forest clearings.

During the course of your research, some field guides or research papers may provide important information on an animal's habitat. Geography books may also provide you with useful general temperature parameters. However, if you have just bought one or more lizards and you need to make some quick decisions as to vivarium design, the general information listed below may help.

Herpetoculturists generally provide a temperature gradient in a vivarium, whereby the temperature is higher under or near a heated basking area and cooler as an animal moves away from the heat source. Generally, herpetoculturists establish gradients along the following guidelines.

Desert/semi-arid area species:
Temperature nearest spotlight: 95 to 100°F (35 to 37.8°C)
Area furthest from spotlight: low to mid 80's°F (27.2 to 30°C)
Nighttime temperatures: 70's°F (21 to 26°C)
Winter: Temperate desert species should be hibernated; otherwise daytime temperatures should be dropped 5 to 10°F (2.8 to 5.5°C), with nighttime temperatures in the 60's°F (15.6 to 20.6°C) for two months.

Temperate species:
Temperature nearest spotlight: 90 to 95°F (32.3 to 35°C)
Temperature furthest from spotlight: high 70's to low 80's°F (25 to 28.3°C)
Nighttime temperature: 70's°F (21 to 26°C)
Winter temperatures: Should be hibernated (brumated); temperature should be 50 to 60°F (10 to 15.6°C) for 2-3 months.

Lowland tropical forest species/
cleared areas/dry tropical forest:
Temperature nearest spotlight: 90 to 95°F (32.2 to 35°C)
Temperature furthest from spotlight: low 80's°F (26.7 to 28.3°C)
Nighttime temperature: high 70's to low 80's°F (25 to 28.3°C)
Winter: Drop temperature 5-8°F (2.8 to 4.4°C) for 1-2 months.

Under canopy/ground level tropical forest species:
Temperature nearest spotlight: 85-90°F (29.4 to 32.2°C)
Temperature furthest from spotlight: low to mid 80's°F (28.9 to 30°C)
Nighttime temperature: High 70's to low 80's°F (25 to 28.3°C)

Montane tropical species:
Temperature nearest spotlight: 80-85°F (26.7 to 29.4°C)
Temperature furthest from spotlight: mid to high 70's°F (25 to 26.7°C)
Nighttime temperature: mid 60's°F to low 70's°F (17.8 to 22.8°C)

The above are general guidelines that should be modified as you find out more information about the species you have purchased.

Annual cooling/hibernation
As a general rule, species from tropical areas should be slightly cooled for one to two months during the winter, and usually kept drier during this period. Imported species from the southern hemisphere may have to be cooled during our sum-

mer. For tropical species, a drop of 5-8°F (2.8 to 4.4°C) is usually adequate. For tropical montane species, a 10°F (5.5°C) drop for about two months is often used by herpetoculturists.   For temperate species, a 15-20°F (7.7 to 10.5°C) drop is used for at least 2 months during the winter.

During this cooling period, animals from tropical countries usually feed less, while animals from temperate countries will not feed at all. Regular monitoring of the lizards is required during this cooler period. Animals that are showing significant weight loss or looking ill should be returned to normal temperatures, and treated if treatment is necessary. <u>Water should always be made available to animals in hibernation.</u>

This is a Parson's chameleon raised by the author from a juvenile. Brief exposures (15 to 20 minutes) to sunlight, either early or late in the day, appears beneficial for this species. Too much exposure to heat and sunlight will kill them.

Heating Systems

Most lizards require heat to fare well in captivity. Failure to provide adequate heat leads to refusal to feed, inactivity, and increased susceptibility to disease. There are several systems for heating lizard enclosures currently available in herpetoculture. Unfortunately, little information is available on the proper use and respective limitations of these various systems. Hot-rock-type heaters are among the most widely sold heating systems and are often marketed as the ultimate heating solution for various reptiles. Unfortunately, they are misunderstood and inadvertently misused by an ill-informed general public. The following information should allow you to make wise choices in your selection of heating systems.

Some General Heating Principles

At the beginning of setting up a vivarium for lizards, herpetoculturists need to address how they are going to generate and control the ground temperature and background air temperature of a vivarium. With large collections, herpetoculturists

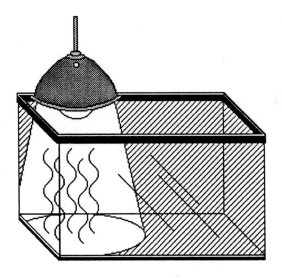

A spotlight placed on one side of a vivarium allows for a heat gradient plus an area for lizards to move away from high temperatures.

often choose to heat the entire room to a level that will be suitable for most of the lizards, using either a central heating system or individual room or space heaters.

For most herpetoculturists, the room temperature will be too cool as a background temperature on a year-round basis, so they will want to set up a heating system to maintain control of the vivarium temperature. As a general rule, heat from incandescent bulbs in reflectors will be the primary daytime heat source; these bulbs are placed over basking sites. For maintaining and being able to control a suitable background temperature, reptile heat strips or heat pads (either with rheostats or on thermostats) are usually installed underneath the vivaria. For nocturnal and burrowing species, reptile heating pads and strips can be used for maintaining a background temperature, and red lights or ceramic infra-red bulbs or temperature-controlled hot rocks are used for generating the high-heat sites. **Note:** At the crux of the thinking about heating for reptile vivaria is the concept of the heat gradient; a range of temperatures and temperature-associated landscaping that reptiles can select from to maintain their optimal body temperature.

A spotlight placed above the center of a small vivarium allows for relatively little unheated space.

Note: Great care and thought should be given to the installation and placement of heating systems. When dealing with electrical heat-generating elements, there is always a risk of fire and electrocution. <u>Think carefully, and follow the manufacturers' instructions and notes of caution</u>.

Incandescent Lighting (Tungsten)

The preferred method of providing a heat source for diurnal lizards is the use of incandescent bulbs (either regular bulbs or spotlights) in a proper fixture, usually with an aluminum reflector with holes near the base to allow for heat dissipation. These lights are typically placed above a screen cover. Some herpetoculturists place them on special stands, such as camera tripods (used with open vivaria). They are also sometimes used inside enclosures, with the bulb encased in a metal wire cage in order to protect the lizards from being burned.

Basking lights are generally suitable for a large number of terrestrial, arboreal and some fossorial lizards that bask. For some nocturnal lizards, such as climbing geckos, low wattage red incandescent bulbs can be a good heat source. However, with most nocturnal terrestrial species alternative heat sources, such as heat strips, are preferred.

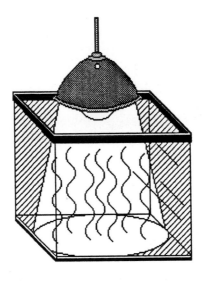

A spotlight placed over a very small enclosure does not create a heat gradient and could even kill lizards by overheating them.

Proper use: Be sure the fixture you choose can handle the wattage and type of bulb you are using or you could have a risk of fire. As with an incubator, the daytime temperature of a vivarium should be calibrated with the aid of a thermometer (preferably digital). By varying the wattage and/or type of incandescent bulbs used, one can achieve suitable temperature gradients within a vivarium. To do this, place the fixture in position over the basking area. Then place the thermometer on the basking area at the location closest to the fixture. Twenty minutes to half an hour later, take a temperature reading. If the temperature is adequate, place the thermometer at an area furthest from the heat source, wait ten minutes and take another reading (this will give vivarium low temperature). If the temperature of the basking area is too high or too low, adjustment can be made using a lower or higher wattage bulb. The wattage of the bulbs may also have to be changed to compensate for seasonal changes in temperature, i.e., higher wattage in the winter and lower in the summer. A light dimmer capable of handling the particular bulbs used can help to establish the desired temperatures. There is also a proportional pulse-controlled thermostat on the market which works very

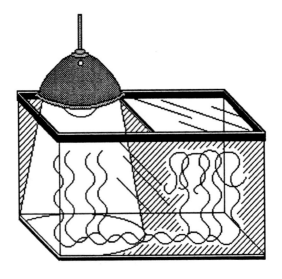

In vivaria with tops partially covered with glass, heat is prevented from escaping through the top and accumulates inside the vivarium. Lizards could be killed as a result of overheating in such a vivarium if an incandescent bulb in a reflector is used. These enclosures are generally not recommended for animals requiring overhead basking sites.

An incandescent fixture with reflector and spotlight. This overhead type of heating is recommended for most diurnal lizards.. Note holes at base of reflector to help dissipate heat buildup.

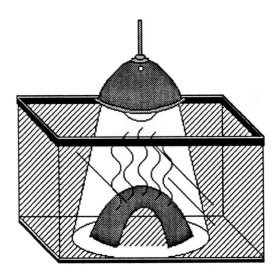

Because heat rises, a shelter heated from above will maintain cooler temperatures inside the shelter than outside. Unlike this diagram, shelters should <u>always</u> be placed some distance away from a basking site.

well for this purpose, thus effectively eliminating concern about changing bulb wattage if the ambient room temperature changes. Vivarium design also affects the temperature gradient. A large vivarium allows for a wide range of available temperatures while a small one, because of its limited surface area, allows for virtually no range. Remember: the lowest possible temperature in a vivarium is roughly equivalent to the ambient room temperature at the same height as the vivarium. As a rule, only low-wattage bulbs (25-60 watt regular bulbs or 50 watt spotlights) should be used with 10 gal ((37.9 lit) vivaria. The use of incandescent light fixtures with standard light bulbs or spotlights as a source of heat is generally <u>not</u> recommended with vivaria smaller than 10 gallons (37.9 liters), because providing a gradient becomes virtually impossible. Many lizards die from overheating as a result of the misuse of incandescent lighting.

Vivaria with covers that are part glass and part screen are not recommended if one intends to use incandescent bulbs as a primary heat source. The glass portion of the cover acts as a heat trap. Unless the vivarium is very large, this can result in

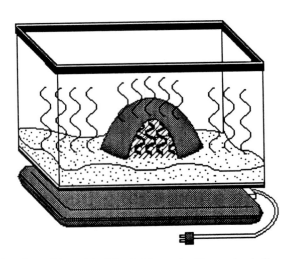

In a vivarium heated by subtank heat strips or heating pads, shelters act as heat traps.

the elimination of a thermal gradient and life-threatening heat could build up. Partially covering the screen top of a vivarium with any solid material may have similar results.

Problems: There is a risk of overheating if a wrong wattage bulb is used. These bulbs are unsuitable for heating very small vivaria because all areas are exposed to the light, resulting in a lack of thermal gradient. There is a risk of overheating in small or partially covered vivaria; also, a risk of fire if the bulbs are placed near flammable materials. They can be expensive if used as the only heat source for a large collection.

Ceramic infra-red element bulbs

These bulbs generate a nice even heat without generating significant light, making them practical for use during both day and night. They are expensive yet long-lived, and may prove particularly useful for heating vivaria at night in areas where rooms get too cold. Care must be given when selecting a wattage (at the time of writing, 60 watt, 100 watt and 150 watt bulbs are available) or you could risk cooking your animal(s). In the author's experience, even the 60 watt bulb is best used

In this photo, the author used two digital thermometers in a vivarium with a subtank heat strip (FlexWatt®). One probe was placed on the surface (right) and one probe in a shelter (left). As should be obvious, shelters can act as heat traps in vivaria with subtank heaters.

with a vivarium at least 24 in. (60.9 cm) long. These bulbs should be used in ceramic fixtures or fixtures capable of handling spotlights; ideally, with reflectors with holes near the base to allow for heat dissipation. Heat buildup in the reflector can shorten the life of the bulb and damage the fixture. A thermometer is required with these bulbs and a thermostat is highly recommended. During the day this bulb should be used in conjunction with fluorescent light. Arrange the ceramic bulb so that the animal(s) cannot make direct contact with it. Place the bulb over basking areas so that plants and/or landscape structures do not get baked. Rheostats and pulse-proportional thermostats can be used in conjunction with these bulbs to adjust temperature.

Problems: There is a risk of overheating if the proper wattage bulb is not selected and if a thermometer or thermostat is not used. **Caution:** The fact that these bulbs do not generate light when they are on can lead to accidental burn injuries.

Hot-Rock-Type Heaters

Hot rocks provide localized heat which does <u>not</u> warm the air in a vivarium efficiently. They are best considered as a secondary heat source for terrestrial reptiles. Also, hot rocks do not create heat gradients. There is an all or nothing situation: often a relatively cool vivarium temperature with a high hot rock temperature. In badly designed pet store setups, lizards sometimes congregate on the only warmth available, the hot rock.

Proper use: These are best used as secondary heat sources for terrestrial lizards, in conjunction with primary heat sources such as incandescent bulbs in reflectors, and for terrestrial geckos at night. Hot rocks should be used in conjunction with a thermometer in order to determine surface temperature. Manufacturers are now adjusting surface temperatures downward. Units with thermostats are preferable to those without, unless one makes an effort to adjust the temperature, e.g., by burying the device under the substrate.

Problems: If used in a vivarium which is otherwise inadequately heated, hot rocks reinforce behaviors such as lizards frequently basking on the hot rock because the rest of the vivarium is too cool. Also, lizards may lie on their bellies against hot rocks for hours at a time. In these cases, if the hot rock surface is too warm, subtle thermal burns or damage to belly scales can result. This type of long-term heat exposure may affect internal organs and fertility of certain lizards, though this has yet to be investigated. At one time hot rocks meant that lizards had a choice of resting on 105°F (40.6°C) surfaces or being exposed to cold. Several manufacturers now offer hot-rock-type heaters which operate within a safe heat range: 80's°F (26.6 to 31.7°C) for some, 90's°F (32.2 to 37.2°C) for others. More expensive versions of hot-rock-type heaters, which include temperature controls, are currently available. These are generally recommended over regular hot rock heaters; adjustment of the surface temperature can be important.

Reptile Heating Strips and Pads
FlexWatt® heating strips
These heat strips are now very popular, in part because of their low cost. At the time of writing they are sold unassembled and require assembly, either by the store owner or the customer.

These heat strips, normally used for heating seed trays in nurseries, come in two widths and two heat levels (a low heat 20 watt and a high heat 40 watt) and are now widely available. When linked to a rheostat, such as a light dimmer, they have proven to be an excellent heat source for reptiles. The strips should be placed in a space underneath the enclosure (for example, along the recessed bottom under a glass tank), making sure that the strip is not crushed by the edge of the vivarium. Flexwatt® is sold by the foot.

Recommendations: This is an excellent and inexpensive source of bottom heat for all-glass vivaria. It creates an even low heat throughout most of the undersurface. For most species these should be used in conjunction with a spotlight over a basking area. Flexwatt® is most useful with recessed glass-bottom or custom-made vivaria, where it can be placed in an air space. A special heat box in which the FlexWatt® is inserted is required for use in vivaria with wood bottoms.

Problems: Note: Flexwatt® should never be used on or applied to a vertical surface; the heat builds to potentially dangerous levels along the upper portion of the strip.

Reptile heating pads
Some of the reptile heating pads are long and narrow enough to warrant being called strips. There are now several brands on

the market. Two popular reptile heating pads are Ultratherm®, which also offers a thermostatic control, and Tropic Zone®, which has received excellent reviews from hobbyists. There are several other brands on the market and others likely to appear in the future. To make a decision, ask the advice of experienced herpetoculturists, whether hobbyists or store owners.

Other kinds of reptile heating pads, including subtank adhesive heating pads, are available. In large sizes and thermostatically controlled, these pads can function in the same manner as heating strips or the heating pads mentioned above. In smaller sizes, these pads have some of the same limitations as hot rocks.

Tetra-Terrafauna® and Zoo Med® are two large companies which manufacture and distribute reptile heat pads, including subtank adhesive heat pads.

Problems: Warm heat pads (particularly adhesive heat pads) without temperature control and in direct contact with the bottom of an all-glass vivarium can cause the bottom to expand and crack. Care must be given when selecting a heating pad size to make sure that a heat gradient is present in the vivarium. Obviously, a heating pad which generates a high heat level and runs the length of a vivarium will prevent the possibility of a cool temperature gradient. With any heat pad, a temperature-regulating device is highly recommended. Read the manufacturers' instructions to lessen the risk of fire or damage to a vivarium.

Heating pads
Common heating pads, available in drugstores, have been used successfully for heating vivaria. This is not recommended and manufacturers warn consumers regarding the risk of fire with misuse. Obviously, common sense is required in order to avoid misfortune.

Proper use: When placing this type of pad under a vivarium, place it carefully, so that the vivarium edges and/or bottom surface do not crush the heating elements or thermostatic controls. These pads should be used only or primarily with a vivarium which has a recessed space underneath. Heat expansion may cause the glass bottom of a vivarium to crack if the control is set too high and the pad is in direct contact with the underside. A vivarium can also be placed on a wood frame (essentially lifting it above the pad) in order to create enough space to prevent these problems from occurring.

Problems: Do not place inside vivaria if the enclosure has a moist substrate. If used inside vivaria, do not cover pad with substrate. Do not use with large lizards, as they may claw through the surface of the pad. Generally, the use of these pads inside vivaria is not recommended. An exception might be for use with a sick lizard. Be very conscious of the risk of overheating and fire.

Room Heaters

Many herpetoculturists resort to the use of electric space heaters in order to maintain an adequate air temperature, particularly if they maintain large collections. This method is effective; it is also expensive and can dramatically increase evaporative rates in vivaria, lowering relative humidity.

Proper use: If one is keeping a large number of vivaria requiring more or less similar ambient air temperatures, electric room heaters can be a simple way to maintain desired warmth in a room. This method is preferred by herpetoculturists with large collections. In winter, space heaters are often the only easy method of maintaining "reptile rooms" at adequate temperatures. They should be used with a backup space heater thermostat.

Problems: The cost of running electrical space heaters is high and does not prove economical unless one has a large number of vivaria. One major concern is the risk of overheated rooms resulting from thermostat variation or failure. A backup thermostat is highly recommended to help prevent this. Another consideration involves placement of the heater and thermostat(s) in the room. During winter, air along the floor is significantly cooler than at mid-room level. If a heater is placed on the floor, particularly if there is a ground-level draft (e.g., a door with a wide space along the bottom edge), the heater thermostat continuously reads a cool floor temperature, remains on and ultimately overheats the room at mid-level and above. In this type of situation, a ten-degree variation could mean a difference between life and death. Several herpetoculturists and commercial breeders have lost their entire collections because of a faulty heater or a mistake in the adjustment of the heater control. Another important consideration with space heaters is risk of fire. Many fires are caused every year by misused space heaters. Place heaters far away from any flammable materials and follow directions very carefully. Once again, backup thermostats are highly recommended.

Pig Blankets

These are large fiberglass-enclosed heating units which are available through feed stores and specialized reptile stores. They are primarily suitable with larger species and in large vivaria. It is important that the heat be controlled with a thermostat because surface temperatures can exceed 100°F. This method is ideal for setting up outdoor enclosures and keeping a heated section or shelter during the cold winter months. They should be used according to instructions to prevent the risk of fire or overheating. Covering the surface of these units is not recommended. Thus these heating units should be used inside a vivarium, exposed and on the surface. They have proven very useful as heat sources in outdoor vivaria.

A hot-rock-type heater. This is useful a as secondary heat source and with some terrestrial nocturnal lizards. Many lizard keepers, particularly pet stores, use hot rocks without providing adequate lighting.

Heating Control &
Monitoring Equipment

The most widely used system for controlling heat in herpeto-culture consists of light dimmers and rheostats. Light dimmers can be attached to lights, as long as directions are followed. Many herpetoculturists have successfully used light dimmers on heat cables and other heating devices, such as FlexWatt®. This is <u>not</u> the recommended usage for these products, and manufacturers do not stand behind their products if they are used in this way, in part because misuse increases the risk of fire. The author is not aware of fire-related problems associated with light dimmers used with heat cables or FlexWatt® heating systems. Nonetheless, connecting these devices to heating systems is done <u>at the user's risk</u>. Other temperature-controlling instruments are available, such as thermostats, though they are more expensive.

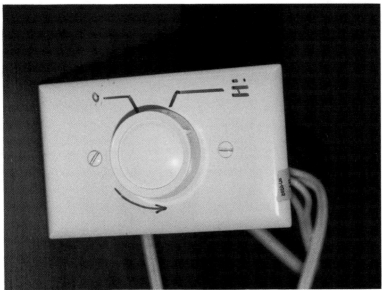

A simple rheostat control (light dimmer) attached to a FlexWatt® heat strip.

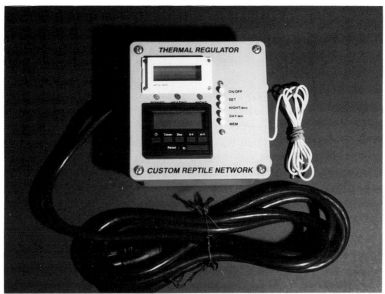

A programmable night/day thermostat system by Custom Reptile Network®.
Both daytime and nighttime temperatures are thermostatically controlled.

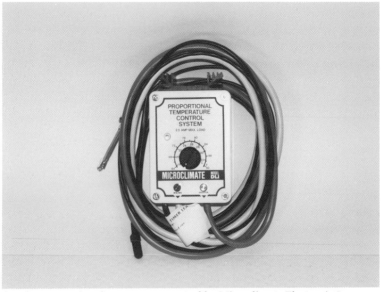

A pulse-proportional temperature control by Microclimate Electronix®.

Thermostats

Most thermostats work by simply switching a heating or cooling unit on or off until the appropriate temperature is reached, and maintaining the temperature within a few degrees, sometimes within one degree, if the thermostat is sensitive enough. Simpler versions, such as wafer-type thermostats used on inexpensive poultry incubators or the thermostatic control of space heaters, require a thermometer to adjust the temperature. You can turn the dial to a certain number, but without a separate thermometer you will not be able to accurately assess the setting of the thermostat. Currently there are commercial thermostats which are manufactured for keeping reptiles (such as Custom Reptile Network®) that allow you to set the temperature, as well as times when the temperature levels must be raised or lowered.

There are also pulse-proportioned control thermostats which, instead of turning a heating device on and off, essentially dim the heat to the right temperature. This type of thermostat is useful for heat cables and strips, for more even heating with incandescent bulbs, and for use in incubators.

Thermometers

Thermometers are essential for properly assessing the temperature in vivaria. The least expensive versions for vivaria are the adhesive thermal-sensitive strips sold as high range thermometers by some distributors. Unlike aquarium strip thermometers which measure a relatively narrow range, high range thermometers indicate lower <u>and</u> higher temperatures, information required in the keeping of many reptiles. However, strip-type thermometers are <u>not</u> very accurate. Standard thermometers, such as wall-hanging thermometers or glass thermometers, can also be used in vivaria. The wall-hanging types tend to take up considerable space; the glass-tube type is sometimes difficult to read.

One of the best thermometers for reptile keepers is the electronic digital readout variety, with a remote probe. An indoor switch position functions to give you a reading where the unit is placed, while the outdoor position gives you a reading wherever the probe is placed. Thus, if a digital thermometer is placed in a room, the probe can provide a reading of the inside of the vivarium. If the thermometer is placed inside a vivarium, the probe could give a reading of the surface of a basking

A programmable digital readout thermometer by Sunbeam®. Maximum and minimum temperatures are recorded. An alarm can be programmed to sound when the temperature goes beyond a set temperature.

This vivarium, designed for dwarf leaf-tail geckos (*Uroplatus fantasticus*), includes wood, cork bark shelters, plants and a varied substrate offering both damp and dry areas.

site. Some of the more sophisticated digital thermometers provide daily minimum and maximum temperature readings; others include an alarm system, which gives warning when the temperature gets too warm or too cool. As should be obvious, these thermometers are invaluable with incubators or wherever careful monitoring of temperature is required. Digital readout thermometers can be purchased through electronic supply stores, such as Radio Shack, and through scientific supply catalogs, such as Edmund Scientific.

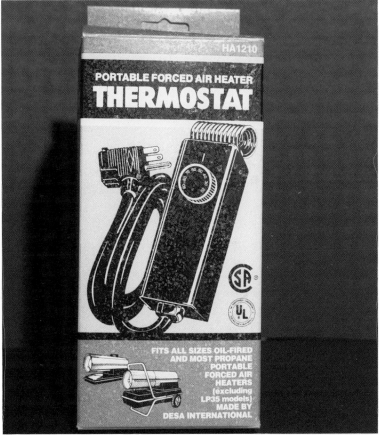

A forced-air heater thermostat, by Desa International, which has been used successfully by herpetoculturists as a backup thermostat for space heaters.

Cooling

Some species of insect-eating lizards require cool temperatures (thus, excess heat may become a problem). These include certain species of true chameleons, some of the Chilean species which require cool night temperatures, and a number of montane species. When in doubt as to why a lizard is not faring well, a cool gradient can be established to allow an animal to select cooler temperatures. Also, if one lives in a warm climate, it may become necessary to lower the temperature in a vivarium at times. The following are a number of different cooling methods used (with varied applications) by herpetoculturists.

Cool Rooms

A commonly used method for keeping lizards that require cool temperatures is to keep them in the coolest area of the house, either in a basement, a garage or a shaded room. In addition, some herpetoculturists insulate a room and install a fan in a partially opened window or in an opening through a side wall, and put the fan on a timer so that cool air blows in at night. During the day, the fan is kept off; the insulation helps retain the cooler temperature. Use a thermometer in order to assess that the temperature is within the desired range. Be aware that during the winter in cold areas of the United States, an unheated basement or garage can have temperatures at, near or even below freezing. This cool room method is commonly used by herpetoculturists who wish to hibernate their lizards.

Cool Packs

Cool packs can be bought at camping stores or supermarkets. The packs are placed in the freezer overnight and then used to maintain cool temperatures for extended periods of time. Purchasing a number of cool packs enables you to rotate them on a 24-hour basis. Use one by placing it under a thin metal container or a shelter, thus creating a cool gradient for terrestrial lizards. Cool packs are also useful when shipping lizards during the hot summer months.

Air Conditioners

Refrigerated air conditioners are the system preferred by most herpetoculturists for keeping species of amphibians and reptiles which require cool temperatures. Usually this means having a room devoted to the keeping of these species. Insulating the room can significantly reduce the cost of running the unit. Some individuals use flexible hose (such as used to vent clothes dryers) to direct the air flow from an air conditioning unit to the enclosures of species requiring cooler temperatures.

Cool-Air Humidifiers and Swamp Coolers

These units cool the air and also increase relative humidity. They can prove useful when only slight cooling is needed. Cool-air humidifiers have been used successfully by chameleon keepers and may prove useful with other species. A hose directing the spray of a cool-air humidifier into a vivarium can be useful for species requiring slightly cool and humid conditions. Adequate ventilation is recommended when using these humidifiers. Cool-air humidifiers should <u>not</u> be used with desert species because high relative humidity may be detrimental to the health of the animals. Air conditioning units are preferable for desert species requiring cooler temperatures. Make very sure you maintain humidifiers according to instructions in order to minimize fungal and bacterial contamination.

Wine Coolers

There are currently available refrigeration units designed specifically for cooling wines. Though relatively expensive, one great advantage of these units is that they are designed for maintaining temperatures of 54-62°F (12.2 to 16.7°C), which coincidentally are suitable for the hibernation of many species. Most units are also available with glass doors which allow for a high degree of visibility. These units allow for the safe hibernation of animals indoors, even in warm climates. Sources for these include mail order catalogs, specialty wine stores and the yellow pages.

Brumation or Hibernation

Most reptiles do not hibernate in the true sense, because even though their metabolism slows down considerably, they often continue to perform various activities, such as drinking and some moving about. For this reason, herpetologists use the words *brumate* (verb) and *brumation* when referring to this process. The author has proposed that the more popular terms *hibernate* and *hibernation* be retained and their definitions expanded to include the following:

Hibernation: 1. A popular term used by herpetoculturists in reference to the winter cooling of amphibians and reptiles in captivity, usually associated with reduced activity and fasting. 2. The process of being subject to reduced winter temperatures and associated limited activity and fasting (used by herpetoculturists with reference to amphibians and reptiles).

Hibernate: 1. A popular term used by herpetoculturists in reference to establishing environmental conditions and exposing amphibians and reptiles to environmental conditions leading to hibernation. 2. A herpetocultural term meaning to undergo the process of hibernation with reference to amphibians and reptiles in captivity.

As a general rule, lizards from temperate climates should be hibernated during the winter for a period of 2 to 4 months. To confirm the need for hibernation, examine the range maps of the species you are keeping and determine the winter temperatures. Lizards from areas where daytime above-ground temperatures are in the 60's°F (15.6 to 20.6°C) or less should be hibernated. Species from borderline subtropical areas should be slightly cooled (5 to 10°F (2.8 to 5.5°C)), with a more significant drop in temperature at night. A slight drop in temperature (5 to 8°F (2.8 to 4.4°C)) during the winter months may increase the chances of breeding certain tropical species.

General temperature guidelines for hibernating/cooling lizards are as follows:

Temperate lizards: 50 to 60°F (10 to 15.6°C). Species from areas where it gets very cold can be hibernated down to the high 40's°F (8.3 to 9.4°C). Do not use spotlights.

Borderline subtropical species: Up to a 10°F (5.5°C) drop during the day while retaining a lower wattage spotlight over a basking area. Use a 10 to 15°F (5.5 to 7.7°C) drop at night.

Subtropical species: 5 to 10°F (2.8 to 5.5°C) drop during the day while retaining a spotlight. Use a similar temperature drop at night.

Note: Hibernation or cooling during the winter should always be accompanied by a reduction in photoperiod to 10-11 hours of exposure to light per day. If you want to keep southern hemisphere species under conditions which simulate their climatic/photoperiodic patterns, then adjust accordingly.

Water

All insect-eating lizards should be provided with some water. As a rule, terrestrial lizards readily drink out of a shallow water container. The height of the water container is important. It should be shallow enough for a terrestrial lizard to see over the rim when in an active position, raised on its four legs. Finding suitable containers may take a little effort. For miniature species, plastic bottle caps or clear plastic casters (for placing under furniture legs) sold in hardware stores may be used. Import stores occasionally offer a variety of small containers that may prove invaluable, from ashtrays to sushi dipping containers. Avoid jar lids that can become corroded. For larger species, ashtrays, plastic food storage containers and pet water bowls (sold in pet stores) work well. Plastic ice cream container tops make excellent dishes for smaller terrestrial lizards.

A number of arboreal lizards drink readily only from droplets of water. The reflection of light against the droplets seems to play a key role in terms of these species recognizing water. Anoles and true chameleons are the best known examples of this type of lizard. In addition, many arboreal lizards that do drink from a water container, would drink more readily from droplets. Many of the geckos, including day geckos, tend to be droplet drinkers.

Misting is the primary method used by herpetoculturists for providing water for arboreal species that drink readily only from droplets. Another method involves using a container (with a pinpoint hole in the underside) which is placed above the vivarium, while another shallow container is placed on the floor of the vivarium. Water is placed in the top container and allowed to drip onto leaves of plants which have been carefully placed above the lower container where the dripping water eventually collects. The lizards are drawn to the water in motion reflecting light. An alternative used by some chameleon keepers is an intravenous drip, such as ones used in hospitals. The unit is placed above the vivarium, filled with purified water, and the drip rate regulated. Here again, a shallow container is placed at the bottom of the vivarium to collect the water.

Quality of Water

In most cases, tap water is adequate for keeping insect-eating lizards. However, many herpetoculturists want to eliminate any possible negative effects of tap water and thus select bottled water for drinking and purified water (which is very low in minerals and other dissolved substances) when misting. Misting with purified water is less likely to leave mineral deposits on the glass. As should be obvious, a high quality of water is important to the health of your animals.

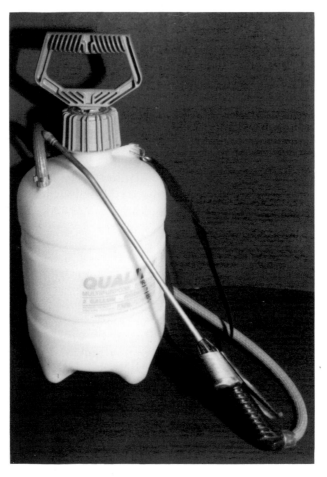

A hand-pump-type sprayer. These will prove invaluable with larger collections when frequent misting is required.

Relative Humidity & Ventilation

Relative humidity is a measure of the degree of water vapor saturation of the air. Measurement is accomplished with an instrument known as an hygrometer. Relative humidity and ventilation are important (though often ignored) considerations when keeping various insect-eating lizards. Desert lizards kept at high relative humidity levels with little ventilation can develop a number of diseases, from respiratory infections and bacterial skin infections to various mycoses (fungal infections). Rain forest lizards kept at low relative humidity levels become stressed, dehydrate rapidly and have shedding problems. It should be remembered that some water loss occurs during protein metabolism and during breathing, when a considerable amount of moisture can be lost to the air, particularly at low levels of relative humidy. Many insect-eating lizards fare well if they are maintained on a dry substrate with water available in a dish; however, there are numerous exceptions.

One key thing to remember is that in the wild, natural shelters usually provide moderate-to-high relative humidity niches. The upper surface of a rock or a piece of wood provides a barrier that reduces air flow under the shelter and thus loss of water to the outside air. Delays in the rates at which rocks heat and cool also result in condensation of water on rock surfaces during the early morning hours. Anyone who has lifted a rock or piece of wood when hunting for reptiles has noticed that the ground is usually damp under the rock or wood. An amphibian or reptile sheltered there does not dehydrate as rapidly and essentially finds itself in a high relative humidity chamber, when compared with the outside air. An animal hiding in such a shelter has access to a level of relative humidity which helps to soften the skin and facilitate shedding. In general, a shelter placed high above the ground provides a lower relative humidity than one on or near the ground.

Some of the challenges encountered in housing certain desert geckos lies not in keeping them dry enough, but in providing enough humidity in their shelters to reduce dehydration and to facilitate shedding. This is the case with frog-eyed geckos (*Teratoscincus*), for example. Tropical forest geckos, such as the bent-toed geckos *(Cyrtodactylus)*, do not fare well at a low relative humidity. Most true chameleons fare best at a relative humidity in the 60 to 80% range.

Methods of raising relative humidity

The easiest way to provide high relative humidity in a vivarium is to design one which contains water, either in the substrate or in a water container. As the water evaporates, the relative humidity increases. If you have a naturalistic vivarium with two substrate layers, one consisting of pebbles for drainage with an upper layer of moist medium, the evaporation of water from the medium raises relative humidity. One of the most common ways of raising relative humidity is to mist the vivarium at least twice daily. The evaporation of droplets raises relative humidity; the substrate also absorbs some moisture and releases it over time. As an alternative, misting systems on timers can be installed by connecting tubing and misters (available for landscape drip irrigation systems) to the plumbing of your home. A drain must be installed at the bottom of the vivarium to allow for drainage of excess water. This is easier than it sounds and is recommended if you are

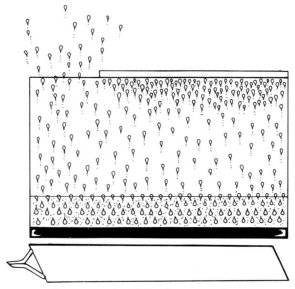

If a substrate contains water, subtank heating causes the water to evaporate. If the top of the enclosure is partially covered, then the water vapor accumulates in the enclosure, increasing relative humidity.

keeping large collections of certain lizards, such as some of the true chameleons; many species fare better when provided with higher relative humidity and with misted water on a twice-daily basis.

Another method of raising relative humidity in a vivarium is to partially cover the top of the vivarium. As water evaporates from the substrate or water container, the rate at which water vapor particles escape the vivarium is reduced and a greater density of vapor accumulates. It is important that only part of the vivarium be covered. If you reduce air flow too much, then accumulating moisture encourages the development of possibly life-threatening fungi and bacteria.

In areas of dry and warm climates, cool-air humidifiers can effectively cool down, as well as raise the relative humidity of, vivaria. They are recommended for the keeping of many tropical forest lizards (including true chameleons) as well as certain geckos (such as bent-toed geckos) in areas with an unusually dry climate. It is important that one carefully read instructions as to the proper maintenance of these humidifiers in order to prevent dangerous bacterial or fungal contamina-

A light placed over a container of water or a subtank heater placed under a container will cause water to evaporate and will increase relative humidity.

tion over time. Many herpetoculturists have had extremely good results using these humidifiers with a number of more delicate species which require high humidity and cooler-to-moderate temperatures.

Methods of lowering relative humidity

If you are living in a high relative humidity climate and are having problems keeping desert reptiles, the following steps help to lower relative humidity. In the room where you are keeping desert reptiles, minimize air exchange with the outside and use a dehumidifier. Refrigerated air conditioners also lower relative humidity. It is also worth remembering that in low (16"H) vivaria in a room with moderate relative humidity, the simple use of spotlights over a vivarium creates a greater evaporative rate or lower relative humidity, particularly if there is no additional source of moisture in the vivarium or the room.

General guidelines for relative humidity

For desert-to-semi-arid species, relative humidity should be less than 60%. Although many desert species tolerate a relative humidity up to 70%, others require a relative humidity of 40%

A digital thermometer with probe and hygrometer (measures relative humidity) sold by Edmund Scientific. The battery on this unit requires frequent replacement.

or less. The relative humidity of deserts varies greatly according to location, from near coastal areas to deeply inland. Get as much information on the species you are keeping as possible. Most lizard species fare well at a moderate relative humidity of 55 to 70%.

Lizard species from tropical forests fare best at a relative humidity of 70 to 80% and some rainforest species may require a relative humidity of 85 to 90%. **Note:** <u>Always</u> provide good ventilation in enclosures with a high relative humidity.

Ventilation

In terms of vivaria, when we speak of ventilation we are not referring of a significant degree of air flow, such as a draft, but rather to areas of air exchange, between air inside the vivarium and air outside the vivarium. With most species, vivaria that have screen tops provide adequate ventilation. However, tall vivaria, in which the area for air exchange (screen top) relative to the total area of the vivaria is small, require additional ventilation on at least one side. An alternative is to use miniature fans, such as ones used for cooling electronic equipment. These can be found in electronic stores (used electronic parts stores are sometimes another inexpensive source). Vivaria that are large, with significant sections of water, also benefit from the use of these fans. One can also create areas of varying dehydration rate, such as might be found in nature when wind provides a greater dehydrating effect at upper tree levels than it does closer to the ground. There is considerable room for experimentation here, particularly in testing for preference when given a range of ventilation levels. Isn't it possible that providing experimental vivaria with different variations might provide a tool for determining environmental requirements of animals for which we presently have little information?

Lighting

For most lizards at least one source of light is required; two are generally preferable.

Incandescent lighting (tungsten)

Standard incandescent bulbs or spotlights (preferable) in a reflector-type fixture is the most effective method of lighting as well as generating heat in a vivarium. These bulbs with reflectors are essential in order to create the temperature gradients required by many diurnal lizards to thermoregulate under vivarium conditions. For primarily nocturnal lizards, such as most geckos, a low wattage red bulb can provide heat without the brightness that these animals typically avoid (see Heating).

Full-spectrum fluorescent lighting

Many herpetoculturists feel that fluorescent full-spectrum lighting, such as Vita Lite®, has positive effects on the welfare of lizards; they typically place one, two, or up to four full-spectrum bulbs running the length of a vivarium. This type of light also allows for the successful growth of plants in a naturalistic

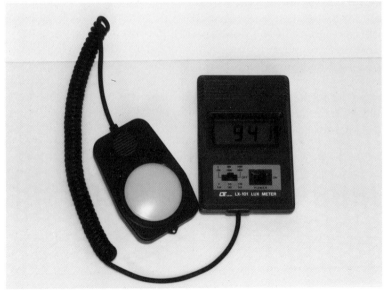

A lux meter to measure light. When designing naturalistic vivaria, these can be used to determine sufficient light for the healthy growth of various plants; also, in the study of lizard behavior in relation to light intensity. This meter is available from Edmund Scientific.

vivarium. The full-spectrum fluorescent bulbs available at the time of writing generate little of the UV-B hypothesized to be required by most lizards in order to synthesize vitamin D3. They do generate a certain amount of UV-A, which many of us suspect has beneficial behavioral/psychological effects, increasing the levels of activity of lizards and also possibly affecting feeding and reproduction. Also, it is possible that UV-A may play a role in vitamin D3 synthesis in lizards.

BL-type blacklights

Many herpetoculturists also recommend the use of BL- (<u>not</u> BL<u>B-</u>) type blacklights for several hours daily for many species of lizards. These bulbs generate several times the amount of UV-A generated by full-spectrum bulbs, such as Vita Lite®, plus little UV-B. Recent studies have shown that several lizard species have ultraviolet-sensitive vision and that UV-A may be important for the herpetoculture of such species as anoles and desert iguanas (Alberts 1993). Successful breeding (high rates of egg fertility and hatching) of Madagascar leaf-tailed geckos *(Uroplatus fimbriatus)* at the Fort Worth Zoo increased dramatically following regular exposure to BL blacklights (Stephen Hammack, pers. comm.). High UV-A levels may have a beneficial effect in terms of calcium metabolism. However, many species of lizards fare well without these lights, particularly if other important aspects of husbandry are attended to, including providing a varied and proper diet (with gutloaded and calcium supplemented insects).

UV-B-generating bulbs

Currently, only a few bulbs generate significant amounts of UV-B. These include UV-B fluorescent sunlamps (FS-type) and self-ballasted mercury lamps. They are not easy to obtain and require certain precautions. In one study on birds (chicks), exposure times (to sunlamps) as short as 30 minutes twice daily was as effective as dietary vitamin D3 supplementation in preventing metabolic bone disease (Wright 1993). With most reptiles, daily exposure time of 5 to 15 minutes is recommended with FS-type sunlamps. Longer exposure times may cause burns and possibly eye damage. <u>An area which offers shelter from exposure to these sunlamps should always be made available during exposure</u>. Mercury lamps generate more moderate amounts of UV-B and can be used for longer periods of time.

Recently, full-spectrum bulbs with higher UV-B levels have been developed specifically for keeping reptiles. They will prove beneficial in allowing animals to synthesize the vitamin D3 required for calcium absorption, without the problems associated with some of the supplements now on the market.

Warning
Protective shields should be used with any BL-type blacklights, FS-type sunlamps, mercury lamps and UV-B fluorescent bulbs, to reduce UV exposure to humans. There is presently some medical concern that humans are being exposed to too much UV from fluorescent light sources. Take good care of your animals; also, take care of yourself and those who live with you.

Red lights
Low wattage red incandescent bulbs will enable you to observe nocturnal animals at night. The nocturnal behavior of many lizards is unknown and much can be learned by observing species active at night with the use of these lights. Red incandescent bulbs can also be used to provide supplemental heat at night. Though the most readily available red bulbs are 25 watts, they are available in higher wattages from stores specializing in lighting and some electrical supply stores.

Sunlight
Insect-eating lizards that bask in the open in the wild, and bask under a spotlight in captivity, can benefit from exposure to natural sunlight, even if only for a total of a few hours per week. Exposure to sunlight is not generally recommended for species living under the canopies of primary forests unless it is done for brief periods, either early or late in the day, when sunlight is steeply angled and the temperature is moderate.

Herpetoculturists fortunate enough to live in areas with good weather most of the year can keep their sun-loving lizards in outdoor vivaria with screen tops, allowing regular exposure to sunlight. In these vivaria, plants should be included to provide shade as well as shelters. As a screen, shadecloth (60%) is recommended for animals that do not bask in direct sunlight/ open areas. During the warm months, herpetoculturists who keep their lizards indoors can transfer their lizards (for a few hours a day) into outdoor vivaria with screen tops, or even screen-sided enclosures, with plants and shelters. Never place glass-sided enclosures in the sun. As sunlight passes through glass, enought heat can be generated to quickly kill your lizards. In the author's opinion, if you can't provide the proper type of outdoor vivarium or a screen-sided vivarium placed in front of an open window (remember sunlight through windows does generate heat), then forego exposing your lizards to natural sunlight. Most species of lizards fare well in captivity under artificial lights. Every year dozens, possibly hundreds, of lizards are killed by well-intentioned owners attempting to provide their lizards with sunlight. Usually the lizards die because of overheating, either because they were kept in glass enclosures or because of failure to provide shade and shelters.

Always provide shelters and shade when exposing animals to direct sunlight. Also, **never** leave purchased lizards in a car in the sun with the windows closed. Infants and dogs have died from heat exposure in such vehicles; so have amphibians and reptiles.

Photoperiod

Photoperiod is the duration of an animal's daily exposure to light. Lizards in the wild are exposed to seasonal variations in photoperiod. In many species this plays an important role in reproduction, particularly with species from temperate and subtropical areas. With most species, herpetoculturists generally set their lights on timers and establish a photoperiod cycle of 13-14 hours of light and 10-11 hours of darkness daily. During the winter/cooling period, the photoperiod is reversed with 10-11 hours of light and 13-14 hours of darkness. By manipulating the photoperiod, herpetoculturists have been able to increase the breeding frequency of certain species. Others have varied the photoperiod to increase the growth rate of baby lizards by creating shorter day/night cycles, e.g., 8 hour days and 6 hour nights to stimulate the lizards to feed more frequently.

Note: Animals living near the Equator are subject to diminished variation in the photoperiod. The further one goes from the Equator, the greater the seasonal photoperiod variation.

Feeding

There is still a lot to learn regarding the diets of lizards in captivity. In fact, relatively little is known of the actual nutritional requirements of most lizard species. The principles of feeding insect-eating lizards employed by most herpetoculturists are the result of relatively few scientific studies, plus considerable experimentation and observation by hobbyists and zoo personnel. Although we don't always know the reasons these methods work, improved health and longevity, as well as increasing success at captive breeding, suggest that the underlying assumptions and principles must be essentially correct.

Feeding is not the only answer

Misconceptions exist as to the role of feeding in relation to an animal's health. By itself, feeding is not enough to assure the long-term survival of a lizard in captivity. Before the issue of feeding is addressed by the hobbyist, other aspects of maintenance must be taken care of, including: selection of an adequate enclosure; a heat source, as well as a heat gradient within the enclosure; the right kind of lighting; the right kind of landscaping; the right level of relative humidity; adequate ventilation, and; water. When conditions are right, the probability of an animal feeding, putting on weight and faring well increases. Feeding will not be a priority for a lizard that is stressed (such as too cold, too warm, too nervous, dying of thirst, etc.).

The staples

In recent years, several species of commercially bred insects have become available in the pet trade, the fish bait trade and through biological supply houses. These should be primary choices as the diet staple for most insect-eating lizards. As a rule, commercially raised insects can provide a good basic diet for a wide variety of these lizards, once the insects are nutrient-loaded and then dusted with a vitamin/mineral supplement before being offered as food.

Other alternatives include field-collected insects and spiders (some Europeans call these "field plankton"), which can be obtained by beating grasses and other plants in fields and/or meadows, and running through with an insect net. But if one is busy and limited for time, commercially raised and readily

> ### The core principle: You are what your prey eats
> A popular nutritional phrase these days states, "You are what you eat." If you are a predator, like a reptile, you are also what your prey eats. Every time a lizard eats an insect in the wild, it consumes the insect, plus any plant or animal contents in the intestine of that insect. This can be seen as nature's way for the lizard to get its meat and veggies all in one neat packet. The contribution of insect gut contents to the diet of an insectivorous lizard should <u>not</u> be ignored. This can be a means of providing important vitamins and minerals, as well as plant compounds, which can contribute to the animal's health, well being and brightness of coloration.

obtainable insects are probably the easiest and most logical source. In addition, you can never be sure that insects collected in the field do not contain agricultural chemicals which could have a harmful effect on your animals.

Feeding lizards right requires forethought, preparation and careful monitoring of one's animals. Illustration by Kevin Anderson.

A Brief Review of Commercially Raised Insects

It is not the purpose of this book to inform people about insect culture. Other books should be consulted for that type of information. The following is information on commercially obtainable insects which should form the staple of your insect-eating lizard's diet. None of these insects should simply be fed to your lizard as you purchased them from a store. The chapter on herpetocultural cuisine gives you information on the right way to gut load these insects.

Gray crickets *(Acheta domestica)*
These are the commercially bred and readily available crickets of the pet trade. They are now carried by most stores which specialize in reptiles. They can also be obtained through fish bait mail order sources. For most lizards these should be the first choice as a staple of an insectivore diet. They can be ordered in a variety of sizes, from pinheads to six-week old winged adults, which means that a suitable size can be obtained for feeding most insect-eating lizard species. Generally, crickets are easily digested by most lizards.

Newly purchased crickets should be kept in plastic terraria and offered a high-quality diet (including cereals, fresh vegetables, orange and carrots) prior to offering them to lizards.

One-week old crickets can be fed and maintained like older crickets, except that the food should be offered in smaller pieces and a finer grind.

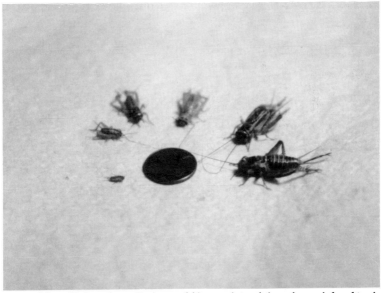

Gray crickets (*Acheta domestica*) are sold in a variety of sizes, from pinhead to six weeks old.

Mealworms *(Tenebrio molitor)*

Mealworms are the most widely sold insects in the pet trade. They can be kept for weeks, stored in a plastic container (with air holes) that is then stored in a refrigerator or a cool area of the house. Serious hobbyists should consider culturing mealworms. They can be maintained and raised in large plastic boxes or tubs filled with an inch of oat bran or corn flour. Before being used, the bran or flour should be baked in shallow pans in an oven at 200°F (93.3°C) for 20 minutes to kill off grain mites. Layers of newspaper or cloth can be placed on top of this layer for easy collecting. Pieces of carrot or squash, as well as banana peel, should be given as a source of water.

One advantage to culturing your own mealworms is that you eventually have them in a variety of sizes to suit your animals' needs, instead of having only the standard medium size offered in pet stores. Two-to-five-week old mealworms can be invaluable for feeding smaller lizards; adult mealworms should only be fed to the larger species of lizard. Another great advantage to raising mealworms yourself is that you are able to offer your lizards "white" soft-bodied mealworms which have just

Mealworms *(Tenebrio)* and king mealworms *(Zophobas)* are good food sources for larger lizards. These worms also need to be gut loaded with a high quality diet prior to feeding.

molted; these are easily digested. Recently, the use of mealworms as a lizard food has fallen into disfavor because the tough chitinous exoskeleton makes them relatively difficult for smaller lizards to digest. All of us who have kept lizards have seen one stuff itself on mealworms one day and regurgitate the entire meal the following day. Feeding smaller mealworms, smaller quantities at one time, and "white" mealworms reduces the incidence of such problems.

As a general rule, mealworms should be offered as part of a varied insect diet., which for many lizard species consists primarily of crickets. But this is not a hard and fast rule; diets should be adjusted according to the lizard species. Generally speaking, larger lizards, whose jaws are capable of cutting through the exoskeleton, fare better with a higher percentage of mealworms in their diet than do smaller lizards. The only suitable mealworms for feeding small lizards are correspondingly tiny ones, whose exoskeleton is likely to be torn by the smaller lizards' jaws; they should also be offered in small quantities.

Mealworms in various stages of development can also be useful as a part of the diet for certain species. With lizards that recognize prey by scent (e.g., some of the skinks), mealworm pupae can be offered as food. For some species of lizards, such as the toad-headed agamid *(Phrynocephalus mystaceus)*, mealworm beetles can also be a valuable food source (though many other lizards will not touch them).

Caution: Do not feed more mealworms than your lizard can eat. Hungry mealworms can injure, and even kill, small lizards that are sleeping on the ground. Mealworms have been implicated in injuries to toes and damage of the cloacal and dorsal-pelvic areas. Feeding only as many as your lizard is likely to eat, plus putting a small piece of carrot in each enclosure (and replacing it as often as needed) can help in preventing this from happening.

King mealworms (*Zophobas morio*)
These resemble mealworms, though they are larger and have somewhat softer bodies. Requiring higher temperatures for maintenance, they are best kept stored at room temperature. They can be maintained like mealworms, except for a greater need for warmth; they also require more vegetable matter as a source of moisture. All that was said about mealworms also

applies here. Some of the larger species of lizards (e.g., adult tokay geckos, basilisks and water dragons) have been maintained successfully long-term on diets consisting primarily of supplemented king mealworms and immature mice.

If these worms are left loose in a vivarium, they can become a problem. They readily eat any eggs they come across; they can also cause injuries (or even death) to torpid smaller reptiles in a vivarium.

Wax worms (*Galleria melonella*)
These are not readily available from most pet stores. They are often most easily obtained through fish bait mail order businesses. They should be stored in pine shavings in a plastic-covered box and stored in a cool area of the house. Wax worms tend to be fatty and are not recommended as a basic diet for most insect-eating lizards. They can, however, serve as a valuable component in a varied insect diet. They can also help lizards put on weight. Many lizards that are reluctant to feed on other insect species will start feeding on wax worms. Though distributors claim this to be a low chitin insect (the implication being it should be easily digestible), wax worms do have an exoskeleton (whatever its composition) which is, in fact, not easily digested by many species of lizards. Thus, they should be offered as food only in small numbers per feeding or one will be faced with the same regurgitation syndrome mentioned regarding mealworms.

As with mealworms, pupae and the adult moths can be a useful food source for some lizards.

Cockroaches (Don't skip this section!!)
There are certain species of cockroaches which can be raised like crickets. They are either wingless or cannot climb glass. A highly recommended and easily reared species, obtainable from some of the biological supply houses is *Blaberus craniifer*. Like crickets, roaches can easily be nutrient loaded. Most people will ignore this section, but for those of you who are dedicated hobbyists, cockroaches can be a valuable food item for some difficult-to-feed species. Try offering them to your reluctant Malagasy leaf-tailed gecko *(Uroplatus sp.)* or Parson's chameleon *(Chamaeleo parsonii)*.

Tropical cockroaches *(Blaberus craniifer)* can be obtained from biological supply houses. They are easily raised in barely moist peat-based potting soil.

Tropical cockroaches can be fed like crickets and are readily gut loaded. They are an excellent food source for those lizards that will accept them, such as Parson's chameleons and leaf-tail geckos.

Wingless fruit flies

Cultures, as well as culture materials, for these tiny wingless flies can be obtained either through biological supply houses or through mail order live tropical fish food suppliers (look for ads in tropical fish magazines). These can be a valuable component in a varied diet for miniature species and their offspring. Larger fruit flies, such as *Drosophila hydei*, can be useful for rearing babies of certain species, including some of the true chameleons and smaller day geckos.

Pink mice

But they're not insects! True, but insect-eating lizards often eat them and they do have a relatively high nutritional value. Pink mice is a term for newborn (hairless) mice. These can be obtained from rodent breeders and through stores specializing in reptiles. Mice are also easily bred in small numbers; a tank containing a group of one male with up to five females could provide at least fifty pink mice a month (more than the average hobbyist would need). In any case, one-to-two-day old mice are eaten by many species of medium-to-large insect-eating lizards. In fact, as far as most of these lizard are concerned, if it moves and it's not too big, then it's probably fair game. Pink mice should be used as an occasional meal, not as a staple diet, for insect-eating lizards. Mice are nutritious, but when only one or two days old they are also calcium deficient for lizards (unless they are offered very soon after removal from the mother). Prior to feeding to lizards, the rumps of the mice should be dipped in calcium carbonate. Do not dip live mice head first or coat them with any vitamin mix as you would crickets. Calcium in the respiratory passages of a pink mouse causes distress and suffering while a rump dipped in calcium does not. Pick or fuzzy mice may be too rich for many insect-eating lizards, and may cause fatty degeneration of the liver if they are fed as a primary diet.

Herpetocultural Cuisine:
Four Steps Toward the Right Way to Feed Insect-eating Lizards

I. Food Selection
This is an important consideration when feeding lizards and one area in which many people lack good judgment.

Size Selection
Errors in size selection of prey are probably the most common in the pet trade. For example, many pet stores selling green anoles *(Anolis)* sell only one size of cricket (five-week old adults) and standard mealworms. Neither of these food items is the right size for the anoles; they are also inadequate for virtually every other small lizard sold. Yet when offered to a hungry anole, it usually goes after the insect and struggles to swallow it. The next day it may seem ill and bloated and often regurgitates. Insect-eating lizards are not snakes and they are not monitor lizards. Most have evolved to eat many small prey

Herpetocultural trick question: Is this the right size cricket for this lizard?
Illustration by Kevin Anderson.

items over the course of a day. You may ask, "What difference does it make?" Well, a large prey has a smaller surface relative to its volume when compared with a small prey. This allows a relatively smaller area for digestive juices to work on. In the digestive tract of a small lizard, a large insect prey item is a big object with a tough exoskeleton. More than likely it was not chewed before it was swallowed. Large prey ingested by an insect-eating lizard may start decomposing before it is digested, and the lizard that has eaten it may become ill and regurgitate the meal.

Another aspect of size selection involves the time it takes prey to pass through the digestive tract. Smaller insects are digested faster and move out of the stomach and through the digestive tract more quickly, thus allowing the lizard to eat again significantly sooner than when it is given large prey. With large insects, sometimes the prey takes up so much room in the stomach of the lizard that even breathing is impaired.

How to gauge the right size insect to feed lizards is learned with experience. As a general rule, the width of the insect should be not more than one third the width of the lizard's head. The length of the insect should be less than one and one-fourth times the length of the lizard's head, and the apparent volume of the insect no more than one third the apparent volume of the lizard's head. Imagine it requiring five insects to fill the belly area of the lizard and choose the insect size accordingly.

What about feeding that green anole?
For sub-adults and adults, three-week old crickets are suitable. These same crickets would also be fed to house geckos, many of the smaller day geckos, the smaller Chilean lizards now being imported, as well as baby green water dragons *(Physignathus cocincinus)*.

Diet selection
For most smaller species of lizards, appropriate-size crickets should be the primary food. If you raise mealworms, smaller "white" mealworms that have just molted can also be used. Mealworms can be a useful food for lizards, as long as the right size is selected. Larger insect-eating lizards should be fed a varied diet of crickets, mealworms or king mealworms, and occasional pink mice. Some species may refuse the above, yet <u>will</u> feed on cockroaches.

Certain species are specialized feeders and require experimentation to determine a suitable diet. For example, the toad-headed agamid *(Phrynocephalus mystaceus)* often refuses most standard commercially raised insects, yet readily consumes mealworms, beetles, and dewinged and stunted flies. There are quite a few species not usually recommended for any but the most devoted and expert of herpetoculturists: lizards that are specialized ant feeders. These include most of the horned toads *(Phrynosoma)*, several of the agamines and the Australian spiny moloch *(Moloch horridus)*, which thrives only on a diet of specific ant species.

II. Food Preparation

Though you might think all you have to do is go to a store, buy a plastic baggy of crickets and dump them into the lizard tank, this approach usually doesn't work, if you want to keep your lizards around for several years. Most people who buy lizards from pet stores seldom keep them for more than a few months. Many imported lizards are not healthy; some are unsuitable for someone who is inexperienced; and also, they are typically not fed in the right manner.

Gut loading

Most commercially sold insects are usually nutrient (including vitamin and mineral) deficient for the purpose of feeding lizards. In brief, their guts are empty and the insect body itself cannot provide all the nutritional requirements of lizards. Virtually all commercially raised insects sold in stores are calcium deficient. They may also be deficient in a number of vitamin precursors and vitamins, including beta-carotene, the B vitamins, vitamin C, and vitamin D3, as well as minerals and trace elements. Plant pigments, which may contribute to an animal's brightness of color, may also be lacking. Indeed, the coloration of many captive insect-eating amphibians and reptiles does tend to fade in captivity.

Solutions for retail stores

One solution for retail stores is to feed an improved diet to insects prior to selling them. This is actually a simple procedure. The following are some recommendations for improving the diet of the most common commercially raised insects.

Offer crickets and mealworms the powdered remains found at the bottom of rodent chow bags or dog chow bags. Flaked baby cereals and ground oatmeal can also be used. Mix in powdered calcium carbonate. For crickets, offer slices of orange as a source of water. For mealworms, offer carrot or squash. In addition to the above, crickets should be offered a variety of greens and vegetables such as: grated squashes, carrots, kale, mustard greens, and/or finely chopped thawed mixed vegetables, on a flat dish in order to prevent any moisture or water from spreading throughout the cricket enclosure.

Food preparation for herpetoculturists

Any hobbyist who buys insects on a regular basis should have plastic containers or bins in which to hold the insects for a couple of days prior to offering them. Some of the translucent plastic terrariums with lids which are sold in pet stores work quite well for this purpose.

The following are methods that work for gut/nutrient loading and vitamin/mineral loading.

For crickets, mealworms & cockroaches

When you first obtain the insects, keep them without food or water for a day. The idea is to make them hungry so that they readily feed on what you are going to offer them. On the next day, offer them one of the following: (1) pulverized rodent chow supplemented and blended with calcium carbonate or calcium gluconate; (2) tropical fish food flakes mixed with high protein baby cereal flakes and calcium carbonate, or; (3) ground oatmeal, barley, other grains, sesame seed with calcium carbonate. Offer this to insects one out of three feedings. The rest of the time, gut load insects with a variety of fresh foods, preferably high in calcium. Vary the vegetables offered: mustard greens, collard greens, kale, cooked green beans, chopped mixed vegetables, Chinese cabbage, grated squashes, grated and/or cooked carrots. Lightly sprinkle greens with calcium cargonate and mix in.

As a source of water, vary the selection by giving slices of orange, the skin of yellow squash, pieces of carrot (grated raw or cooked).

Feed the insects to lizards on the following day.

Optional food preparation

Prior to the vitamin/mineral supplementation and offering of insects to lizards, many specialized hobbyists do the following:

<u>Crickets</u> are caught individually and the "thighs" pinched, either with tweezers or by hand, which causes the crickets to drop their hindlegs. These crickets cannot jump out of the feeding dishes or move around as actively, thus slowing the rate at which vitamin/mineral supplement coating is lost.

<u>Mealworms</u> are pinched hard at midbody with fine tweezers or between thumb and forefinger. The result is partial paralysis of the back half of the mealworm. Here again, escape from a feeding dish is prevented. Another consideration is that pinched and injured mealworms that escape do not usually survive. In the case of king mealworms in particular, this would be desirable in a vivarium where lizards are breeding.

One technique used with lizards that recognize prey by scent is to crush the heads of mealworms with tweezers. The result is a mealworm that "smells" right but doesn't move. This works well with lizards like baby monitors or Indonesian blue-tongue skinks *(Tiliqua gigas)*. These animals can spend so much time thrashing and eating a single active mealworm that by the time they return to the dish, the others may have all escaped.

By placing crickets in a dish with pinched-off hindlegs to prevent or slow down dispersal in the vivarium, the lizard keeper will increase the effectiveness of his supplementation regimen.

All of this may sound cruel to insects, but what a lizard does is not going to be any better. We're dealing with predators and we must decide between the welfare of predator lizards and that of insect prey.

III. Vitamin/Mineral Supplementation

When you don't have the time to nutrient load insects, the very least you should do is this next step.

With proper gut loading of insects and with the opportunity for exposure to natural sunlight, minimal supplementation will be required when feeding your lizards. Most of the commercial lizards breeders that keep their lizards outdoors and feed their insects a high quality diet use little or no supplementation. Under the above conditions, supplementation once a week with powdered calcium carbonate is usually all that is required. Recent research seems to indicate that it is probably best to avoid vitamin D3 supplementation if lizards are regularly exposed to sunlight (Dr. Gary Ferguson, pers. comm.).

For lizards kept indoors with no exposure to sunlight, vitamin/mineral supplementation will have to be adjusted to one's procedures, with regards to gut loading of insects and

Vitamin/mineral coating of crickets prior to feeding.

maintenance systems. If you use a strong UV-A- or UV-B-generating bulb (UV-generating bulbs are due to appear on the market in the near future for use with reptiles), then with a proper gut loading regimen, calcium supplementation once or twice a week should be all that is necessary. There is still some question as to whether BL-type blacklights, which generate relatively high levels of UV-A, yet low levels of UV-B, may actually enable lizards to absorb calcium. The distance from the bulb to the animal is probably a critical factor. Unfortunately, we do not know enough about calcium metabolism in lizards (which appears to vary from species to species) to have pat answers to questions about the best feeding procedures.

If there is no exposure to high UV-A- and UV-B-generating bulbs, then calcium/vitamin D3 supplementation once a week is recommended with most species of lizards, as long they are fed high quality, gut-loaded insects. With hatchlings and subadults, calcium/vitamin D3 supplementation twice a week is recommended.

Without proper gut loading of insects, it will be necessary to resort to commercial vitamin/mineral supplements to correct deficiencies associated with nutrient-poor food insects. This is not without risk, because most commercial reptile vitamin/mineral supplements are based on modified bird formulations that have not been supported with research. As a result, many of the commercial vitamin/mineral supplements tend to be high in vitamin A and, in some cases, vitamin D3. Other vitamins are also probably not present in the right proportions. Ideally, a formulation should be developed that allows for regular dusting without the risk of overdosing; thus, it should be a very dilute vitamin/mineral supplement. A mixture of one part commercial vitamin/mineral reptile supplement with two or three parts calcium carbonate, used to dust food insects once a week, will be adequate for most adult insect-eating lizards. For immature animals, a twice-a-week supplementation schedule is recommended. Depending upon the species, this will have to be adjusted. Obviously, an adjustment will be necessary if an animal shows signs of metabolic bone disease. It is worth noting that because most lizard buyers will not provide the right kind of lighting and very unfortunately will not feed their food insects a varied diet, vitamin/mineral supplementation will probably be critical for most lizards sold in the pet trade to fare well long term. One of the most common diseases in captive lizards, metabolic bone disease, will be easily prevented with proper suppplementation.

In spite of some of the recently uncovered problems with current commercial vitamin/mineral supplements, there is no doubt that the practice of vitamin/mineral supplementation by hobbyists has contributed significantly to the successful captive breeding and rearing of many lizard species.

Supplementation schedules

Many hobbyists vitamin/mineral supplement the insects they feed at every feeding, but it <u>is</u> possible to give too much supplementation. The result can be mineralization of subcutaneous and visceral organs, usually as a result of calcium deposits. This type of metastatic calcification can result in premature death. Another problem caused by oversupplementation is vitamin A and/or vitamin D3 toxicity.

We do not yet have clear guidelines as to the actual vitamin/mineral requirements of most lizard species. As a rule (until better information comes along), the diet of juveniles (because of their rapid growth rate) should be supplemented more often than that of adults. Most herpetoculturists vitamin/mineral supplement the diet of juveniles every 1 to 2 feedings. Once the animal is mature and its growth rate has slowed down, supplementation is usually cut down to <u>every third or fourth feeding,</u> in order to reduce the probability of metastatic calcification. Another choice is to supplement the insects fed to adult lizards with a vitamin/mineral powder in one feeding per week, and with calcium carbonate in a different feeding each week. When breeding lizards, herpetoculturists usually increase the schedule of calcium/vitamin D3 supplementation or calcium carbonate for females, thus making sure that enough calcium is available for the formation of adequately calcified egg shells. During the breeding season, gecko breeders usually dust insects with calcium carbonate or a calcium/vitamin D3 supplement at every feeding.

Calcium supplementation of geckos

Many gecko breeders use special methods to provide large amounts of calcium to their animals. One method is to make available at all times calcium carbonate or calcium gluconate powder or RepCal®; place powder in a jar lid or small dish set

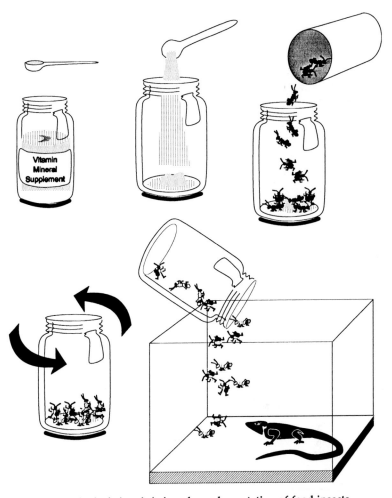

A common method of vitamin/mineral supplementation of food insects.

on the substrate or on a platform in a gecko's vivarium. With species that are known to ingest sand regularly, such as *Teratoscincus,* calcium carbonate is added and mixed into the sand substrate. With species that are very prolific and have high calcium demands, such as the Madagascan ground gecko *(Paradoeura picta),* calcium in liquid form or mixed with a watered down baby food may be administered individually with an eyedropper or syringe. Liquid calcium carbonate can be obtained by prescription from a pharmacy.

Some type of vitamin/mineral supplementation is recommended for the long-term survival of most insect-eating lizards in captivity.

Until better methods are available, pet stores recommending that you buy vitamin/mineral supplements (even for keeping the inexpensive green anole *(Anolis carolinensis)* that you have just bought) are <u>not</u> just out to make a buck; their suggestions are based on the current practices of most lizard keepers.

Special techniques
In order to help determine their contribution to the overall health and captive breeding of insect-eating lizards, three vitamins are currently being experimented with by some breeders: beta-carotene (a vitamin A pre-cursor), vitamin C and vitamin E.

One method hobbyists use to administer beta-carotene and vitamin E is to purchase gelatin capsules of these products at health food stores and to offer (once a week) one or two crickets which have been hand dipped (the dorsal part of the insect) into the spilled contents of a capsule and then into a mineral/vitamin mix prior to feeding. Beta-carotene is also available in a powder that can be added to the vitamin/mineral mix.

For administering vitamin C, crystal vitamin C is purchased at a health food store, then placed in a small mortar and crushed with a pestle. Vitamins can also be crushed by placing them between two pieces of cardboard and pounding them with a hammer. A small amount of the finely powdered vitamin C is added to the vitamin/mineral mix for coating of insects.

The following are some of the benefits attributed to the use of these vitamins by some herpetoculturists.

Beta-Carotene may play a role in increased reproductive success, improved coloration and prevention of eye and respiratory disorders. A current view of many experienced herpetoculturists is that beta-carotene, in the form of grated carrots fed to insects or as a supplement, is probably the best and safest way to assure that lizards get adequate amounts of vitamin A. The current view is that formed vitamin A, because of the risk of overdosing, may be harmful to certain species and may possibly impair long-term, multi-generational breeding. Hypothetically, if given beta-carotene a lizard would convert to vitamin A only as much as it needed.

Vitamin C is present in the diets of most reptiles; it is probably obtained primarily from the gut contents of prey. A small amount of vitamin C in the diet may help prevent mouthrot (stomatitis). Other benefits have yet to be determined.

Vitamin E may improve the likelihood of reproductive success with reptiles. In veterinary medicine, vitamin E in the diet has been shown to reduce or prevent steatitis, a condition resulting

Many herpetoculturists use a mortar and pestle to pulverize medications and vitamin/mineral supplements. Coarse commercial supplements can be ground finer. Human vitamin/mineral supplements in tablet form can be pulverized, e.g., vitamin D. Make sure the vitamin D is vitamin D3 (cholecalciferol) and not vitamin D2 (ergocalciferol). Calcium and beta-carotene, also available in tablet form, can be pulverized in like manner. Mortars and pestles can often be found in import stores.

from excess consumption of unsaturated fatty acids. Typical symptoms of steatitis include massive accumulations of altered fat, as well as the development of lesions under the skin and throughout the abdominal cavity.

The above supplementation techniques are experimental and any claims as to possible benefits remain speculative.

IV. The Right Way to Serve Lunch

Most hobbyists, after swirling insects in a jar with vitamin/mineral mix, simply dump crickets, mealworms, etc., onto the floor of the vivarium. However, if you have only a few lizards and you put in too many insects at one time, the uneaten ones will scurry about the tank, losing their vitamin/mineral coating. When you offer more insects than are needed at a single feeding, the excess crickets hide; mealworms burrow in the substrate. Later, your hungry lizard eats these escapee insects, probably nutrient depleted and without the vitamin/mineral coating.

The author has heard many stories of hobbyists who swear that they methodically vitamin/mineral coated their insects when feeding baby lizards and "they developed rickets anyway." The cause is invariably the wrong calcium/phosphorus ratio or inadequate amounts of vitamin D3 or (quite often) inappropriate feeding methods that allowed the introduced insects to lose their vitamin/mineral coating.

When feeding insects to lizards, the first rule is: <u>Don't offer them more than they will eat at one feeding</u>. After a period of time, the appropriate number of insects to be fed at each feeding can easily be determined. Some people with large collections have a very methodical way of feeding in such a way that each vivarium gets a specific number of insects at each feeding.

The second rule is: <u>Introduce coated insects in a feeding dish</u>. The challenge is finding the right kind of dish. Unfortunately, no dishes sold in the pet trade, including the standard plastic watering dishes, are designed for feeding insects to reptiles. To find the right dish will require a trip to an imported goods or department store in search of small porcelain or glass dishes. For small lizards, import stores often sell small sauce dishes that work quite well. Finding the right dish is not easy. It should to be high enough to prevent the insects from crawling out, and yet not so high that, after you sink the dish in the ground medium of the tank, the lizards can't see the contents. Note: Crickets without hind legs and pinched mealworms will usually not be able to easily escape from smooth glass- or porcelain-sided dishes.

Forceps feeding

Many lizards learn to take food offered them from forceps. One advantage of this type of feeding is that you can control the quantity of insects offered and eaten by a specific lizard during a feeding. In a community situation, where certain lizards may be dominant over others, this allows you to feed each lizard individually and assure that all are adequately fed. Forceps-feeding is also useful in controlled experimental situations. Forceps can be purchased from medical supply houses and specialized reptile dealers. One disadvantage to their use is that lizards will sometimes inadvertently clamp down on the forceps itself, at the risk of damage to the mouth and the possible development of stomatitis (mouthrot).

Feeding tubes

Another method is to create an insect feeding tube or jar. This can be made of bamboo, PVC pipe or an empty coffee can. A feeding tube is essentially a container with a top to allow for the placement of insects and supplementation inside. About 1/4 in. (6.4 mm) from the bottom, two 3/8 - 1/2 in. (9.4 to 12.7 mm) holes are drilled. Small corks that fit these holes should be purchased so that the holes can be plugged at will.

Open the lid of the tube and add a layer of vitamin/mineral mix that reaches the bottom of the punched holes. Place a number of coated insects inside the container. Close the lid, place inside the vivarium and remove cork plugs from the holes. The insects will struggle to get out, getting even more coated with the mixture. Eventually they will emerge, one at a time, from the container. Over time, lizards will become conditioned to feeding from the tube/container and wait to grasp an insect as it exits the feeding tube.

Feeding schedules

Feeding schedules should be adjusted to the age and growth rate of your animal. Most juvenile lizards have a very rapid growth rate and thus require frequent feedings to build muscle and skeleton. They should be fed every 1 to 2 days. After

Forceps feeding of crocodile lizards *(Shinisaurus crocodilurus).* This method allows for controlled feeding of insect-eating lizards. Care must be taken that the lizard does not bite down on forceps and injure its teeth or mouth.

A feeding tube. Crickets are placed in the open top, become coated with the supplementation mixture inside, and then crawl out of the tube into the enclosure. Illustration by Glen Warren.

growth slows down and levels off (between one and two years in most species), feeding should decrease to three times a week. Females in breeding, particularly those laying several clutches of eggs during a breeding season, should be placed back on a one to two day schedule. Care should be given to avoid obesity. A plump, rotund lizard is not a healthy lizard. Such animals may be incapable of breeding and may be destined to a shortened lifespan. Use your good judgment and/or seek the advice of an experienced herpetoculturist.

Hypervitaminosis A

Dr. Larry Talent, of the University of Oklahoma, and Dr. Gary Ferguson, of Texas Christian University, have been conducting research on the effects of specific vitamins on certain species of insect-eating lizards. Preliminary results of their ongoing research suggest a possible relationship between vitamin A, vitamin D3, and calcium metabolism. Excess vitamin A in commercial reptile supplements may have a negative effect with several species of insect-eating lizards, notably certain species of true chameleons (i.e., C. johnstoni and C. pardalis), day geckos and fat-tail geckos. Because of an interrelationship between vitamin A, vitamin D3 and calcium, it appears that too much vitamin A may deplete calcium reserves, resulting in symptoms of metabolic bone disease. Other effects of hypervitaminosis A include excessive shedding and eye problems. Some of these effects can be offset by increasing the amount of vitamin D3, but there is a risk of administering too much vitamin D3. Unfortunately, many of the reptile vitamin/mineral supplements presently available contain many times the amount of vitamin A required by most lizards. For species with low vitamin A tolerance, these vitamin/mineral supplements may prove detrimental over time. With vitamin A-sensitive species, some herpetoculturists choose not to use any commercial vitamin/mineral supplements, and instead simply use a vitamin D3 and calcium supplement. Other vitamins are provided through careful gut loading of the insects being offered. Gut loading of insects with beta-carotene is the method most often used by herpetoculturists for supplying vitamin A to their insect-eating lizards. Care is given not to feed insects a diet which is high in formed vitamin A, but instead to feed a diet low in vitamin A, including fresh vegetable matter, ground rodent chow and flaked baby cereal. Another method is to mix one part of a commercial supplement with 2-to-5 parts calcium carbonate. Hopefully, commercial vitamin/mineral supplements with lower vitamin A levels will become available in the very near future.

Feeding Female Lizards During Their Breeding Cycles

For female lizards, the demands of reproduction mean the investment of considerable energy in the production of eggs. In addition, several species of insect-eating lizards lay multiple egg clutches, further taxing a female's energy reserves. Because the synthesis of egg shells requires calcium, significant demands are placed on the calcium reserves of gravid females. In captivity, failure to provide adequate calcium can result in soft- or thin-shelled eggs, less resistant to trauma and disease. There is also evidence that the nutritional quality of the diet offered a female lizard can affect the size of eggs and the quality and quantity of food reserve available to the embryo (in the yolk). Thus, it is important that care be given to offer breeding and gravid females a high-quality diet which is rich in calcium.

Sizes and types of foods offered to gravid females will also have to be varied. Because the developing eggs may take up a significant portion of the abdominal cavity, the digestive organs may be compressed, thus making feeding on large prey, or on a large volume of prey items, impossible. Gravid female lizards will usually feed on smaller prey and ingest a smaller total volume of prey per feeding. Offering smaller prey more frequently is highly recommended at this time. Poor health and inadequate diet are believed to be associated with an increased risk of egg binding in gravid females.

Fungi and fungal toxins

It is very important that all food fed to insects be fresh and changed regularly. The enclosures insects are housed in should be kept clean. There is some evidence that insects that have consumed moldy food can harbor fungi and fungus-derived toxins which could prove harmful or fatal to lizards. In the case of some fungal toxins (e.g., aflatoxins), the effects may be cumulative, so keep food insects in a meticulous manner. Offer fresh food. Make sure it is not moldy.

Other Foods
Plant matter

Several species of insect-eating lizards will also feed on plant matter. Well known examples are some of the larger agamines (such as bearded dragons and water dragons), basilisks, several species of skinks, plated lizards, several species of swifts, several species of teiids (such as ameivas), etc. Several gecko species will also feed on baby foods or nectars.

The best way to find information as to whether a species also consumes plant matter is to consult the available literature. Another way is to experiment. Offer a dish with a variety of finely chopped vegetables or fruits and observe which ones the animal seems to prefer. Good choices are:

Leafy greens such as kale, romaine lettuce, mustard and collard greens
Finely chopped mixed vegetables (fresh or frozen and thawed)
Grated squash
Grated carrots
Finely chopped green beans

"And today my little chirpers, squash and corn pancakes with flower petals and chicken titbits, a la Lacertoni, of course." Chef Carlo Lacertoni, author of *Gourmet Food Preparation for Your Food Insects* and *Smooth Passage: Feed what you feed before you feed.* (Illustration by Kevin Anderson.)

Peas
Banana (small amounts)
Chopped apple
Peach

For day geckos *(Phelsuma)*, prehensile-tailed geckos *(Rhacodactylus)*, Madagascar velvet geckos *(Homopholis)* and others, banana or peach baby food with a little calcium carbonate mixed in will be readily accepted. You can try this with other geckos or lizards and observe their responses.

Pink mice

Many large insect-eating lizards can be given newborn to fuzzy mice as part of a varied diet. Some of the larger geckos, skinks, plated lizards, girdle-tailed lizards, agaminae (including bearded dragons and green water dragons), basilisks, European giant legless lizards, galliwasps, dwarf monitors, etc., will accept larger mice. Once again, you may have to experiment. As a rule, with species that are primarily insect-eating, it is not a good idea to convert them to a primarily unweaned-mouse diet; it may be too rich (high protein and high fat) for long-term good health. Weight gain and softer stools will often be noticed

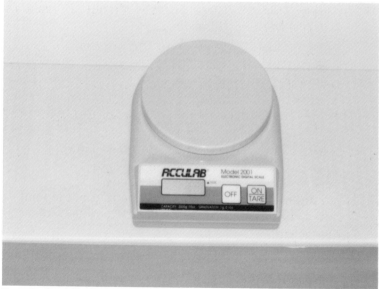

Records should be kept on the lizards you are keeping, including weight, length, dietary and behavioral notes. Relatively inexpensive and accurate electronic digital scales are obtainable through scientific supply catalogs.

on a diet containing too high a percentage of unweaned mice. The author recommends that mice make up no more than 10-to-25% of the diet of insect-eating lizards.

Freshness of supplements

It is better to purchase smaller amounts of a fresh supply than a large amount of vitamin/mineral supplement that might last you a long time. A large container of vitamin/mineral supplement opened frequently (or with contents exposed to the air or high temperatures) will deteriorate over time until you are no longer able to assess the effectiveness of the vitamins. Fat-soluble vitamins, such as vitamin A and vitamin D3, are prone to rapid deterioration. It is best to read labels for expiration dates, buy smaller volumes, keep supplements in a cool place, and keep containers sealed tightly between uses.

Meats

Generally, many lizards that are frequent tongue flickers will feed on non-moving food. Fine strips of lean beef (e.g., flank steak) or beef heart and cooked chicken will be taken by these species, but these foods should be supplemented with a calcium/vitamin D3 supplement. For lizards that will eat them, these foods can make up one component of a varied diet. Until research demonstrates differently, they should not make up more than one-fourth of the animal's diet.

A Sample Gut Loading Diet for Insects

Fresh foods (2X/week)	Grains/Seeds (1X/week)
Kale	Baby cereal flakes
Mustard greens	Ground rodent chow
Collard greens	Ground oatmeal
Carrots	Ground barley
Green beans	Sesame seeds (sm. amount)
Grated squashes	(high calcium/high fat)
Orange slices	

Note: Add finely powdered calcium carbonate to above. Vary the diet of insects and the diets of lizards.

Relative Surface-to-Volume Ratios

An important principle in herpetoculture is that of relative surface-to-volume ratios. Briefly, this principle states that, all other things being equal (e.g., same species, body proportions, etc.), the larger an object or animal, the smaller its relative surface-to-volume ratio; conversely, the smaller an object or animal, the greater its relative surface-to-volume ratio. To make this more understandable, let us take as an example the relative surface-to-volume ratios of two cubes. One cube has one foot sides and the other has two foot sides.

The surface of one side (a) of a cube is side x side (a x a = a^2). To obtain the total surface you multiply the surface of one side (a^2) by the number of sides (6).

The volume of a cube is side x side x side (a x a x a = a^3) .

In the case of cube A
  Surface of one side is 1 ft x 1 ft = 1 sq ft
  Total surface is 1 sq ft x 6 = 6 sq ft
  Volume is 1 x 1 x 1 = 1 cu ft
  Surface-to-volume ratio is 6-to-1

In the case of cube B
  Surface of one side is 2 ft x 2 ft = 4 sq ft
  Total surface is 4 sq ft x 6 = 24 sq ft
  Volume is 2 x 2 x 2 = 8 cu ft
  Surface-to-volume ratio is 3-to-1

In terms of herpetoculture, this is important because smaller animals have a greater surface-to-volume ratio. Thus, they heat up and cool down faster than large animals. Also, they can usually digest their food faster. Their rate of metabolism is higher, partially because the surface-to-volume ratio applies internally, as well as externally. Small animals dehydrate faster than larger animals. As a rule, disease will tend to overtake smaller reptiles in less time than larger reptiles.

The same principle applies to crickets. Small crickets have a higher surface-to-volume ratio than large crickets. When coating small crickets, the amount of vitamin/mineral supplement can be proportionately two or more times the amount adhering to large crickets. This can be beneficial in some cases,

Herpetocultural trick question: "I take cricket A and cricket B and put them in a jar with supplement. Which one will be covered with more supplement?" (Illustration by Kevin Anderson.)

"Mommy, I put Little Charlie out so he could get some sun like Big Charlie, but look, he's all dried out and dead!"

"How many times have I told you to think surface-to-volume ratio, think surface-to-volume ratio, think surface-to-volume ratio?" (Illustration by Kevin Anderson.)

but in others it can lead to hypervitaminosis, such as hypervitaminosis A, for example (which is proving to be a significant problem with some species).

This principle can also be applied to vivarium design. Stratifying space in a vivarium essentially subdivides a large volume into a number of smaller ones and thereby increases the available surface area.

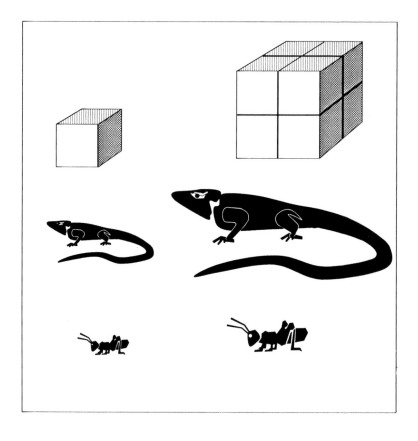

A cube with 1 in. sides has a 6 sq. in. surface area and a 1 cu. in. volume, or a 6-to-1 surface-to-volume ratio. A cube with 2 in. sides has a 24 sq. in. surface area and a volume of 8 cu. in., or a 3-to-1 surface-to-volume ratio. All other things considered equal, a small object has a greater relative surface area than a larger one. Thus, baby lizards heat up and cool down faster than adults. Proportionately more vitamin/mineral powder can adhere to small crickets than to large ones. Small prey insects are digested more quickly than larger ones.

Handling

Most lizards should be kept in vivaria in which they are observed. As with keeping tropical fish, the animals' appearance, aesthetics, and behaviors are primary sources of enjoyment derived from keeping them. Many lizards are quite fast and will tend to scurry when given the opportunity. Only some of the medium-to-large species, which tend to be relatively calm and not subject to sudden panic or flight behaviors, are suitable for handling or as pets. Among these are some of the terrestrial geckos, including the popular leopard geckos and fat-tail geckos. Other geckos, such as prehensile-tail geckos *(Rhacodactylus)*, can also be handled for short periods of time. Australian dragons of the genus *Pogona* are <u>very</u> docile and among the best lizard pets one can own. Calm when handled, they are recommended for children, as long as there is some adult supervision. Also, plated lizards, particularly *Gerrhosaurus major*, can be handled. The author has seen very tame plated lizards carried on the shoulders of their owners. Some of the larger skinks (such as Schneider's skinks *(Eumeces schneideri))*, anguids, as well as larger lacertas (such as the green lacerta *(Lacerta viridis))* do tolerate some handling.

As a rule, larger lizards, which are not prone to panic/flight behaviors, are those most recommended for handling. Observation and experimentation will aid in determining the degree to which a lizard can be handled, but if having a lizard as an easily handled pet is a primary goal, consider some of the species mentioned, particularly the inland bearded dragon *(Pogona vitticeps)*. Another rule is that <u>no</u> hatchling or juvenile lizards should be handled while they are small. Immature lizards are much more prone to flight behaviors and are often more delicate than adults. For example, although adult bearded dragons are highly recommended for handling, young dragons are somewhat delicate and should <u>not</u> be handled while they are small. Leopard geckos, when they are small, can be feisty and prone to sudden dashes, seldom remaining calm in one's hand. In contrast, with regular handling many of the adults make relatively nice pets.

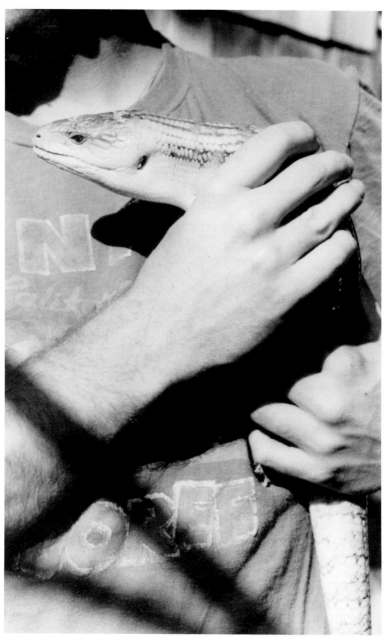

Northern blue-tongue skinks *(Tiligua scincoides intermedia)* are moderately large, hardy and easily kept lizards (omnivores that feed on food obtainable at the supermarket). They are ideal for those wanting a tame lizard that can be handled. This ten-year old animal was raised by the author.

When experimenting with handling a species, <u>always</u> do so in a room with little furniture, and the door kept shut. Make sure there are no open areas allowing for escape outside, or furniture that can be climbed under and into. Escapes under and into the mechanism of a stove or refrigerator could present a serious problem. It is also a good idea to handle lizards on or over a table, rather than simply standing up. A table will minimize the distance that a lizard can fall if it should escape your grasp during handling.

Dream or nightmare? Obesity and fatty livers are common problems with "babied" pet lizards. (Illustration by Kevin Anderson.)

DISEASES & DISORDERS

Insect-eating lizards, being for the most part of small-to-moderate size, will generally be more difficult to treat than larger vertebrate-eating or vegetarian lizards. For this reason, the importance of disease prevention cannot be over-emphasized.

Captive Conditions & Disease
Environmental factors such as temperature, humidity, substrate type and landscaping can provide conditions which lead to disease. Social stress factors, such as bullying by conspecifics and/or competition for food or vivarium niches, can also be important factors leading to susceptibility to disease-causing organisms. Always evaluate environmental and social conditions when an animal appears sick. Make necessary changes to rectify problem situations.

The following are essential guidelines for disease prevention:

1.   Carefully select animals prior to purchase. Avoid thin, listless, or sick-looking animals. If several specimens in a given group of imported animals appear ill, even the healthy-appearing animals may have been infected with various disease organisms by other members of the group.

2.   Whenever possible, purchase captive-bred or -raised animals; these are less likely to be parasitized or diseased.

3.   Quarantine all new animals for at least 30 (preferably 60 to 90) days prior to introducing them into a vivarium with other lizards. If possible, quarantine them in a separate room. Adopt maintenance procedures to help prevent infection of healthy animals. Healthy animals should be cared for first, followed by potentially healthy animals in quarantine; sick animals should always be maintained last. At the end of the maintenance schedule, you should wash thoroughly with a disinfectant, such as Betadyne® scrub, and then avoid contact with healthy animals the remainder of that day. Any tools should be disinfected and a different set of tools used with each respective group of animals. Many people ignore the quarantining of

animals and later deeply regret this when most of their collection becomes ill and/or is wiped out. Please heed this advice.

4. Deparasitize animals. Internal parasites play an important role in the inability of imported animals to establish to captivity. Many imported insect-eating lizards harbor nematodes, tapeworms, and/or flagellate protozoans. Many insect-eating lizards are small and treating them for parasites (in terms of dosages and administration) can present challenges. As a rule, the easiest way to administer medications is orally. With very large groups of very small lizards, it is sometimes best to weigh the entire group, finely pulverize the appropriate amount of medication with a mortar and pestle and use the crushed medication as a powder to coat food insects, basically placing the insects in a container with the pulverized medication, gently swirling the insects in the mix and offering the coated insects to the lizards. The dosage will be variable and inaccurate but this method is sometimes the best recourse for treating large groups of inexpensive lizards. Panacur® (fenbendazole) in liquid form, appropriately diluted, can easily be administered to small species with an eye dropper (see Klingenberg 1993).

An accurate weighing instrument that measures in fine increments (such as a triple beam or digital scale), and knowing how to properly dissolve medication and determine dosage, will be essential for treating individual lizards. Because of miscalculation, inexperienced herpetoculturists sometimes administer up to ten times the recommended dose of a medication. In terms of parasite treatment, because many small insect-eating lizards are relatively inexpensive, the veterinary cost of treating them or checking them for parasites can exceed many times the initial cost of the lizards. Furthermore, there is no guarantee that having spent all that money, the lizards will survive.

5. Keep animals in properly designed vivaria that meet the essential requirements of the animals. Inadequate environments can significantly stress animals and contribute to their decline and susceptibility to disease. Inappropriate or inadequate temperature, relative humidity, water availability, landscaping and/or social conditions are all factors which can contribute to stress and to failure of an animal to adapt to captivity. It is important to maintain setups on a regular basis and to provide a high-quality diet, along with high-quality water.

6. Monitor animals daily and visually check them to discern their health status. Always segregate and quarantine any animals which appear ill or stressed as soon as they are noticed.

Veterinarians & Insect-Eating Lizards

Generally, insect-eating lizards that appear very sick do not survive, even if you take them to a veterinarian. Like birds, lizards often do not display obvious symptoms until they are very ill. The earliest symptoms tend to be so subtle that one often does not notice them or simply considers the animal to be having a bad day. "Sherman's not feeling very peppy today and hasn't eaten anything." The problem is that the next step can be a very sudden decline. "Sherman's lying on the bottom of his cage and barely keeps his eyes open and hardly moves at all." At this stage one may panic and call for an appointment with a veterinarian, hoping for a miracle. In most cases, the miracle doesn't happen. Sherman checks out, and ends up with the winged lizards in saurian heaven. You end up thirty-five or more dollars poorer and disappointed in the veterinarian who couldn't save your lizard.

How does one make decisions about taking a lizard to a veterinarian? The author's advice is as follows:

1. Locate an experienced reptile veterinarian <u>before</u> you need one. Good sources of information for reptile veterinarians in your area are herpetological societies, herpetoculturists (particularly commercial reptile breeders) and reptile dealers. Another option is to look in the yellow pages and find a veterinarian that advertises that he or she is experienced with reptiles or exotic animals.

2. The best time to consult a veterinarian is soon after purchase when the animal is healthy. Prevention is always the best course with reptiles. Imagine that you have just purchased a relatively valuable lizard, such as a Parson's chameleon, a green tree monitor, or an adult double-crested basilisk. You want to know whether the animal is healthy and whether it harbors parasites. In this situation, you should definitely consult a reptile veterinarian and have a general examination plus a fecal exam performed. As an example, green tree monitors are imported and often arrive with protozoan infections. Untreated, these animals will decline and eventually die. Treated, they will often thrive and live for many years. In the case of small

and inexpensive lizards, you need to carefully weigh financial considerations, because the costs of a veterinary visit and parasite check can amount to several times the cost of the animal. If you are careful in your selection, there is a good chance that your animal will be relatively healthy. The decision is up to you.

3. If one of your lizards appears ill but still has some vigor, waste no time in taking it to a qualified veterinarian. Early diagnosis and treatment will be critical if it is to survive. When you bring your animal to a veterinarian, be candid about what you can or cannot spend. "Doctor, I want to let you know that I can only afford to spend up to x amount on this animal." This allows a veterinarian to provide you with options for treatment. For example, a veterinarian may say that he or she suspects that your animal has x parasites, and that tests to determine this will cost x amount. He or she may suggest that if you want, instead of administering the tests, the veterinarian will treat the animal based on assumption and then wait for an improvement. In other cases, a veterinarian may state that the cost of treatment would be very prohibitive, would not necessarily succeed, and that it might be better to euthanize the animal or let the disease follow its course. Ultimately, the decision as to what to do and what you can afford is yours alone.

4. If the lizard is small, common, and relatively inexpensive, and is looking very ill (listless, keeping eyes closed, and/or very thin with eyes barely open), resign yourself to the fact that your lizard is unlikely to survive. The cost of veterinary treatment will ultimately be much higher than it would be to replace the lizard, and the animal is probably going to die, no matter what you do. When small lizards go downhill, they go quickly and can suddenly (even within a few days' time) reach a point of no return. Save yourself the money, the energy and the grief. If you have a good rapport with a reptile veterinarian, he or she will probably give you the same advice or charge you a minimal fee for a quick prognosis of the situation. If you have a valuable animal or an animal that you dearly care for, if the animal still has a little spunk and if you can afford to spend the money (knowing that it may well be of no use), then you may want to consult an experienced reptile veterinarian.

5. Veterinarians are often quite effective in treating a lizard that has injured itself, but otherwise appears quite healthy. A key factor here will be the cost involved. The author's advice is to decide what you can reasonably afford or, better yet, what you want to afford.

An Overview of Some Common Diseases in Insect-Eating Lizards
External parasites
Ticks

Some species of wild-collected insect-eating lizards harbor ticks. These external parasites can be seen as flat scalelike creatures, either imbedded between scales or embedded in the soft skin of armpits, groin, and/or eyelids. Tweezers should be used to remove individual ticks. Using a cotton swab dipped in rubbing alcohol, applying it to the body of the tick and waiting five to ten minutes before tweezing will facilitate removal. The author has seen imported true chameleons that harbored such large numbers of small ticks in the armpits that removing all the ticks at one time could have caused serious trauma. Rubbing alcohol was applied to all tick bodies but they were removed a few at a time over a period of several days.

Mites

These small beadlike parasites are not common in fine-scaled insect-eating lizards or burrowing insect-eating lizards. The author has seen them on some of the larger skinks and on species with large overlapping scales, such as swifts (*Sceloporus*). The presence of white flecks (mite feces) on the skin of an animal is a reliable indicator of mite infestation. Examining an animal with a magnifying glass or running a moist paper towel across the skin of a lizard (then checking the towel visually) are two other methods used to determine the presence of mites. The treatment of mites in insect-eating lizards can be difficult. If seen on a lizard with fine-grained skin, such as a day gecko (infested by mites from other lizard species kept in dealers' facilities), the best solution is to thoroughly wash or spray the animal with water until it is clear of mites (in a location where the mites can be flushed down a sink). Then keep it in a relatively bare enclosure until it can be ascertained that all mites are gone. Relatively few mites will live and breed on insect-eating lizards with fine, non-overlapping scales. With some desert lizards, particularly species that burrow, keeping them on a fine silica sand will result in a gradual decrease and eventual elimination of mites. Some species, such as certain swifts, can harbor difficult-to-eradicate species of mites. One method of killing these mites consists of placing in the enclosure (30 gallon or larger) a plastic container with perforations (such as a deli cup), inside which is a 1/2 in. x 3 in. (12.7 x 76.2 mm) section of a pest strip impregnated with 2.2 dichlorovinyl dimethyl phosphate. The enclosure should be partially covered, but an opening should be left to allow for some air flow. Mites will usually be killed within 12 hours. (Note: Some lizards may be sensitive to pest strips.) The animal(s) should then be removed from the existing enclosure; the enclosure should be thoroughly washed and disinfected with a 5% bleach solution. All landscape materials should be disposed of or disinfected with a 5% bleach solution. The lizards can then be placed back into a newly designed setup. Note that reptile mites usually lay their eggs in the areas surrounding their host, rather than on the host. Monitor the animal carefully and repeat treatment if it is needed. An alternative treatment, which is still considered experimental and which has not been tested on lizards, is the use of Ivermectin in a spray form. It has proven quite effective on snakes. A Triclorfon spray has also been shown to be effective with various reptiles but has proven toxic in geckos (see Klingenberg 1993 for more information). Fortunately, most of the insect-eating lizards sold in the pet trade do not usually harbor mites.

Skin diseases and shedding problems

A variety of skin diseases will be found among insect-eating lizards; these will range from bacterial infections to certain skin cancers. Many skin diseases are associated with improper environmental conditions (such as too much moisture, which can lead to bacterial or fungal infections). Others, including certain types of cancers, are transmitted. Fortunately, most insect-eating lizards are not prone to skin diseases (see Frye 1991 for more information).

Shedding problems

Improper environmental conditions are the primary cause of shedding problems in insect-eating lizards; usually inadequacy in terms of relative humidity, substrate and/or landscaping. For example, many geckos, including terrestrial species, will shed more easily if relative humidity is 50% or more. In the wild the relative humidity in shelters is consistently higher than in the open. Another cause of shedding problems is illness. Sick lizards are often too weak to adequately perform shedding behavior and may manifest shedding problems. In those cases, if the skin is loose and lifting from the body, the lizard should be assisted by manually removing the shed. The cause of illness should be diagnosed and the lizard treated. Unusually frequent shedding is often associated with illness.

In captivity, another cause of shedding problems in species with a low tolerance to excessive vitamin A levels is hypervitaminosis A. Some of the day geckos, including *Phelsuma standingi*, fat-tail geckos *(Hemitheconyx caudicinctus)* and some true chameleons (e.g., *C. pardalis* and *C. johnstoni*) are sensitive species in this regard. Switching to supplements with a low A content will usually reverse the situation.

Metabolic bone disease/calcium deficiency

Symptoms of calcium deficiency were common among insect-eating lizards before the use of vitamin/mineral supplementation of food insects. Fast growing hatchlings, newborns and breeding females are particularly susceptible. With proper husbandry this disease is easily prevented. In insect-eating lizards, metabolic bone disease/calcium deficiency will be caused by the following:

1.   Lack of calcium in the diet.

2.   Lack of vitamin D3 which is necessary for calcium to be absorbed.

3.   Inadequate calcium-to-phosphorus ratio. The ratio of calcium to phosphorus in the diet of lizards should be 2 parts calcium to 1 part phosphorus.

4.   Unavailability of natural sunlight to allow an animal to synthesize its own vitamin D3. In captivity this is usually remedied more or less effectively by providing vitamin D3 orally through food-insect supplementation. An alternative is the use of UV-B generating bulbs.

5.   Excessive amounts of vitamin A in at least some species.

Symptoms of calcium deficiency/metabolic bone disease include:

1. Flexible lower jaw, skull bones or limbs. Foreshortening of lower jaw.

2. Deformities of the jaws, back bone and tail.

3. Inability to feed.

4. Hind limb paralysis, listlessness.

5. Fibrous osteodystrophy resulting in swollen appearance of jaws and/or limbs.

6. Decalcified eggs in gravid females.

Treatment includes daily oral administration of calcium and vitamin D3 supplements, plus short exposures to sunlight or another UV-B source. In severe cases a veterinarian can administer an injectable calcium.

Injuries

Minor injuries, including skin lacerations, should be first disinfected with Betadine® solution and, followed by application of an antibiotic ointment such as Neosporin®. Deep injuries, including lacerations that do not close, deep bites, or punctures wounds, will require similar treatment and may also require stitches as well as the administration of injectable antibiotics. A reptile veterinarian is best qualified to perform such procedures. Any injured animal should be removed from the conditions, either physical or social, that led to the trauma. It is best kept on a simple and relatively sterile substrate, such as newsprint or brown butcher paper, while recovering.

Swellings and lumps

Lizards may develop swollen areas; commonly toes, but jaws, limbs and sometimes the cloacal area can be affected. These swellings often are due to infections which will have to be incised, emptied, flushed and treated with antibiotics. In some cases, lumps will turn out to be tumors.

Consulting a qualified veterinarian is recommended in most cases. Filthy and overcrowded conditions increase the probability of infections, so correcting environmental conditions is very important.

Internal parasites

This has been covered in other sections. As a rule, all wild-collected animals will be infested with internal parasites. Parasites with direct life cycles (such as pinworms and hookworms) can, under captive conditions, increase to life-threatening levels; they should be treated. Certain species of insect-eating lizards, such as some of the true chameleons, are infested with such large numbers of nematodes that captive stress quickly leads to an imbalance between parasite and host. For this reason, many herpetoculturists treat (or have treated) any new animals with Panacur® (fenbendazole) at a dosage of 75 mg/kg. Insect-eating lizards can also have parasites for which they are not the normal host. These parasites will eventually burrow through the host and get lodged underneath the skin or sometimes in the lungs. Some of the nematodes and plerocercoid tapeworms fall into this category.

Many imported lizards from tropical areas may be infected with flagellate protozoans because of the filthy conditions in which they are maintained in dealers' compounds. Routine treatment with Flagyl® (metronidazole) at 50 mg/kg has proven beneficial for many of these species. For more information on parasites and parasite treatment, see Klingenberg 1993 (a work geared to herpetoculturists) and Frye 1991 (more technical).

Failure to feed

If a lizard is active and healthy and yet fails to feed, then you need to consider the following: Either you're not offering the proper diet or certain environmental or social conditions are wrong. This means you will need to do additional research on the species, experiment with alternative diets, and possibly modify environmental conditions. In cases involving social factors, you may encounter situations with dominant individuals intimidating more submissive animals. On occasion, introducing an established animal that eats with a non-feeding animal can help elicit feeding.

A lizard that is failing to feed is most often ill. Listlessness and weight loss are also associated with failure to feed. Check for external parasites, particularly mites. Observe the lizard for gaping or forcible exhalation (respiratory infection). Check the inside of its mouth for excessive mucus, lumps, areas of redness, or accumulations of caseous matter. Check stools to see if they are runny. Consider having a stool check done. If the lizard is still active, then assist feeding by placing a pre-killed insect in the animal's open mouth. With some species a liquified diet can be offered using a large syringe to dispense the food orally. This diet might include: baby food, such as banana, mixed with chicken baby food plus water plus liquid vitamins, or; a high-calorie paste diet, such as Pet Kalorie®, mixed with water. Many geckos and frequent tongue-flicking species will lap liquid diets from a feeding syringe. Ensure®, a high calorie liquid diet available in drugstores, will work well. If the lizard is weak, food should be administered directly into the stomach with a feeding tube attached to a feeding syringe. Such a lizard might be unable to swallow food; in this case to assist the animal by placing food in its mouth will simply hasten its demise. After a period of trying to swallow the food, the lizard could die with the pre-killed insect in its mouth or throat. Recommended procedure in such a case is to offer a liquified food via a feeding tube. In order for the lizard to survive, the cause of the disease will have to be determined and the animal treated appropriately.

Respiratory infections

In smaller lizards, the most obvious symptoms of respiratory infection are labored breathing, gaping, forced exhalations, inactivity and failure to feed. If the lizard is held and the end of the thumb used to gently press up against the throat, mucus may be seen emerging through the nostrils. In the earliest stages, raising the temperature to 88-90°F may allow the animal's immune system to overcome the infection. In serious cases, an antibiotic must be administered; however, antibiotic treatment of a small lizard may prove difficult. If one is willing to pay the cost, a reptile veterinarian should be consulted. Note: Be aware that the smaller the lizard, the quicker its rate of decline and the smaller the chance that veterinary treatment will be successful.

Sudden weight loss in imported lizards

The sudden decline usually associated with weight loss in imported lizards is often caused by internal parasites having a negative impact on the host, following exposure to prolonged stress (usually environmental). Rehydration of the animals on a twice-daily basis is recommended, e.g., by administering electrolytes orally with an eye dropper (Gatorade® can help or infant electrolytes, such as Pediolite®). The animals should be checked for internal parasites and treated as needed. Inadequate environmental conditions, viral diseases and social stress can also lead to sudden weight loss.

Gastroenteritis

Infections of the GI tract are common in imported lizards. Symptoms of gastroenteritis include runny or discolored stools, bloody stools, and unusually smelly stools. These symptoms are usually accompanied by weight loss, listlessness, and loss of appetite. The recommended course of treatment is to have a fecal exam performed by a veterinarian and to treat the animal accordingly. Flagellate protozoans are a common cause of gastroenteritis in imported lizards. These are easily treated with Flagyl® (metronidazole) at a dose of 50 mg/kg, administered orally; repeat in four days. Coccidia and *Pseudomonas* are two other common causes of gastroenteritis in captive lizards.

Salmonellosis

Salmonellosis is a disease caused by bacteria of the genus *Salmonella*. This disease can be transmitted from infected animals to humans. In humans it causes nausea, vomiting and diarrhea; in severe cases it can cause paralysis, coma and (rarely) death. Young children, immuno-suppressed adults and older people could die if infected with salmonella. Some cases that have attracted great attention lately are associated with green iguanas. When one considers the number of these animals imported each year (hundreds of thousands), the number of people infected has been relatively <u>very</u> small.

To prevent any problems with salmonella, be sure to adopt the following guidelines:

1. Do <u>not</u> allow children to handle lizards without supervision. Lecture them about <u>not</u> putting hands in their mouths when handling or after handling lizards. Anyone and everyone should <u>always</u> wash hands thoroughly, preferably with a bactericidal soap, after handling lizards.

2. Do not practice maintenance procedures in areas, or with utensils, used by humans. This includes not cleaning out enclosures in the kitchen, not allowing animals on kitchen counters or in sinks or bathtubs, and not using human food utensils for animal maintenance. If this is done, all areas and utensils should be washed and disinfected after each exposure.

3. If your animal shows symptoms associated with salmonellosis (listlessness, loss of appetite, weight loss and wet, loose stools), have a veterinarian perform a fecal exam. If infected, one course is to euthanize the animal; another is to attempt treatment. Failure to notice symptoms of salmonellosis does not mean that your animal is not infected, since many reptiles can be symptomless carriers. If you are concerned about your children and/or immuno-suppressed individuals, then have a fecal exam performed as a routine procedure.

In conclusion, be aware that salmonellosis contracted from insect-eating lizards is very rare and that even people in the pet industry, handling thousands of lizards per year, are not infected. In fact, members of the pet industry are often surprised when incidents of salmonella infection are reported. Most cases of salmonellosis contracted by humans from lizards are associated with green iguanas. With a minimum of common sense (e.g., washing hands after handling), there is very little risk of contracting salmonella from lizards. You probably have a greater risk of contracting salmonella from poorly cooked eggs or chicken than from lizards. Be aware, and don't be misled by media sensationalism.

There are signs that certain health departments and the media are trying to generate a salmonella scare with regard to lizards and other reptiles. Animal rights organizations will be waiting to take advantage of every opportunity, and every bit of information that will allow them to pursue their dangerous and destructive agendas, agendas that could ultimately result in all of us no longer being permitted to have animals of any kind in our lives. (See Marquardt, et al., 1992.)

Egg binding
Gravid female lizards, particularly imported species, can suffer from egg binding, also known as egg retention. There are various causes of egg binding in lizards. One common cause is the absence of a suitable environment for the laying of eggs. Providing shelters over a container of a moist medium, dumping freshly dug soil in which a preliminary burrow entrance is created by hand, laying a slab of wood over a portion of moist substratum, and placing vertical egg-laying sites, such as hollow bamboo stems are all methods that have been used by different herpetoculturists to encourage females to lay their eggs. Egg-bound females that are off feed, but still appear

healthy, should be given Ensure® (available in drugstores) plus calcium with a feeding syringe once or twice daily. As soon as females seem to become even slightly weakened and listless, contact your veterinarian if the animal is important enough to you that you want her to survive and/or possibly save her eggs. The usual veterinary procedures involve either administering vasotocin, a hormone which causes contraction of smooth muscle, or surgical removal of the eggs. If an animal dies, the eggs can sometimes be saved if surgically removed soon after death (preferably within a few minutes).

Intestinal Prolapse

Either enteric disease or, in some cases, accumulation of fecal material that contains large chitinous parts can cause an eversion of the terminal intestinal tract. If noticed early, the everted section can be gently reinserted (reverted) into place. If not noticed, the everted section will swell, become damaged and eventually dry out or become infected. With valuable lizards, immediate attention by a qualified veterinarian is recommended.

Illustration by Kevin Anderson.

When You No Longer Want to Keep Your Lizards

Many aspects of life, such as a career change, going away to school, moving, changes in family structure, etc., can leave you unable to continue to keep your animals. The first course of action in such a situation is to find out if there are friends or other hobbyists who might be interested in the animals you own. Advertising in herpetological society newsletters or in the pet section of the classified ads of your newspaper may help you find interested buyers. If you are in a hurry, the easiest course is to sell your animals back to the store where you purchased them or to make arrangements over the phone to sell them to one of the many specialized reptile dealers. Remember that dealers will usually pay a wholesale price for animals, approximately one-half to one-third of the price a customer will pay for them (stores have many expenses and the prices paid for the animals take into account such factors as rent, employee wages, insurance, cost of maintaining animals and making a profit). If you cannot sell your animals, then consider giving them to a store, herpetological society adoption committee or auction, or the science departments of some of your local schools.

Do not under any circumstances ever release your animals into the wild. The release of non-native species into the wild can jeopardize native wildlife, as well as our rights as herpetoculturists to keep non-native species. For all our sakes, and for the sake of the animals, do not ever do this. Resorting to the recourses mentioned above you should be able to find alternative homes for your animals.

Shipping & Receiving

Mail order makes up a significant portion of the reptile trade. Thousands of lizards are shipped every year, across the United States and in some cases abroad. The first step in the process is to make sure that any required paper work is taken care of; the second is to verify the legalities of shipping the animals. For example, lizards from California cannot be legally collected and sold for commercial purposes. In some states permits may be required to own certain lizards.

How to ship

Lizards in the United States are shipped primarily by air freight or by overnight Express Mail. Businesses should check with U.P.S.; they may also allow overnight shipment of lizards. Overnight shipping is recommended only during times of the year when temperatures are mild, neither too cold nor too hot. Checking weather reports for the areas of departure and destination is recommended whenever you are shipping animals. Never ship lizards during unusually cold periods or during heat waves.

Call the post office to determine whether they provide overnight express mail service to your intended shipping area. If shipping by air, call the air freight office to determine whether the particular airline you have in mind will transport live lizards, what flight your animal(s) should be on and at what time you should be at the airport (typically the airlines recommend that you be there about two hours before flight time).

Packing: Lizards should be shipped in a polyurethane foam tropical fish shipping container with a cardboard box exterior. You may have to contact tropical fish stores to obtain these containers. You can also make a polyurethane foam-lined cardboard box. Just buy an insulation foam panel at a large hardware store and a utility knife. Panels can be easily cut out and taped together with duct tape, inside a cardboard box.

Using a knife or a screw driver, poke one hole through each side of the box, making sure it goes through both the cardboard and polyurethane foam liner. This is required for adequate ventilation. As should be obvious, making the holes should be taken care of before the animals are introduced.

The lizards, depending on size, should be placed in cloth bags or in cardboard containers such as milk cartons. Add some shredded newspaper or paper towel to the bag or container, since the lizard may be bounced around during transport. Make sure you punch holes in the boxes or cartons for ventilation. Cloth bags can be sealed with tape or the ends tied in a knot or fastened with rubber bands (be careful of the lizards). Milk cartons can be stapled or taped. Cardboard boxes can be taped. Next, place the bag(s) or carton(s) in the shipping box and use crumpled newspaper to prevent shifting during the journey.

During cool weather, chemical heat packs can be used to keep the lizards warm. The packs are usually taped to the inside of the shipping box, either to the top or sides. They should <u>not</u> be placed in direct contact with either bags or cardboard boxes because of the possible risk of overheating. During unusually warm weather cool packs can be used, placed in such a way that they are not in direct contact with the inside containers. Some herpetoculturists place them in cardboard boxes or in plastic containers with multiple holes punched in them.

You should now be ready to seal the shipping box. Many herpetoculturists place an invoice or care instructions inside the box at this point. Others will tape them in an envelope to the outside. Any required paperwork is best taped to the outside.

Close the box and seal with packing tape or duct tape. Make sure that the ventilation holes are not covered. Label the box indicating who it is being shipped to and the shipper. <u>Always indicate the phone numbers of both persons</u>.

On top of the box you should also indicate the following:

Harmless Lizards
Number of Animals
Genus/Species

Recommended additional labeling:

On sides:

> **Keep Right Side Up** △
> **(with an arrow leading up)**

On sides and/or top:

> **Keep at 70 - 80°F**
> **Live Lizards**

Insurance: It is a good idea to insure animals for their full value when shipping, particularly if they are valuable. Unfortunately, airlines do occasionally lose shipments.

Notify the person receiving the animals by telephone, giving the time you shipped the animals and their estimated time of arrival. Ask that you be notified if the animals do not arrive as expected.

Receiving animals

When receiving animals by air, it is a good idea to open up the shipment at the airport to verify the state of the animals if there has been a problem and/or delay with the shipment. Do this very carefully to prevent any possibility of escape. You simply want to ascertain whether the animals are alive or not. If the animals arrive dead, this can be verified by airline employees and a claim form filed. This procedure can facilitate your being credited/compensated by the shipper. The airlines will often replace the animals for the invoiced/insured value plus air freight costs, if it can be determined that the death of the animals was due to their negligence, e.g., a shipment gets lost for several days during cold weather. The above procedure does not apply to Express Mail shipments, because most commercial shippers will not guarantee live arrival when animals are shipped via Express Mail. Do not open animal shipments inside a post office.

> **Laws**
> Check state, local and federal laws before collecting, receiving or shipping United States species. If shipping to another country, check CITES regulations and the Endangered Species Act. Write or call United States Fish and Wildlife for necessary information.

A five-lined skink (*Eumeces fasciatus*). This United States species will fare best in a forest-floor-type vivarium, including a slightly damp substrate with a dry surface and basking sites. The female will guard an egg clutch. The young have a bright blue tail. Photo by Jim Bridges and Bob Prince.©

Timor monitor *(Varanus timorensis)* eggs hatching. This primarily insect-eating species has been imported in small numbers from Indonesia. It is semi-arboreal and should be provided with climbing areas and shelters in the form of cork bark rounds (tubes). There are increased reports of the captive breeding of this species and several other small monitors. Keep in a tropical forest vivarium with moderate relative humidity. Photo by Jim Bridges and Bob Prince©.

A Moorish gecko *(Tarentola mauritanica)*. Imported with regularity from Israel in recent years, this species needs a desert vivarium with vertical rock slabs or large rocks (primarily a rock/wall dweller). It can be kept with other desert species within the same size range. Males kept together will fight and kill each other. Check imports for parasites. Photo by Jim Bridges and Bob Prince.©

A giant frog-eyed gecko *(Teratoscincus keyzerlingii).* This is one of the most beautiful of the terrestrial geckos. They should be kept in desert vivaria with subtank heat strips plus both standard and humidified shelters. If cooled during the winter, they will breed readily. Best kept in groups of one male with two or three females. If kept under red light at night, you will have the pleasure of observing their interesting behaviors. Photo by Jim Bridges and Bob Prince.©

A white-striped gecko or palm gecko *(Gecko vittatus)*. This is a beautiful species that is easily kept and bred in a tropical vivarium with moderate humidity. Check imports for parasites. Photo by Jim Bridges and Bob Prince.[©]

A green lacerta *(Lacerta viridis)*. These lizards have been seasonally imported in some numbers for the past few years. Males have larger heads and femoral pores. In breeding the throat and parts of the lower jaw are a brilliant blue. They should be kept in a desert vivarium. They will fare poorly and die if they are kept on damp substrate. Do not keep males together. This species is best kept in pairs or trios (one male with two females) by themselves. This is a hardy and underappreciated species in the United States. Photo by Jim Bridges and Bob Prince.[©]

A blue-tailed tree lacerta *(Holaspis guentheri)*. This is an African arboreal lacertid that is seldom available to herpetoculturists. Photo by Jim Bridges and Bob Prince.[©]

A common flat rock lizard (*Platysaurus intermedius*). These attractive lizards are saxicolous (rock dwelling) and will thrive in a well-designed desert vivarium. Unlike other cordyline lizards, the members of the genus *Platysaurus* are egg-layers. Photo by Jim Bridges and Bob Prince.©

A four-lined Malagasy plated lizard (*Zonosaurus quadrilineatus*). The author has successfully kept this species outdoors in the San Diego area and indoors in desert vivaria. It behaves somewhat like a skink, and spends a great deal of time burrowed in the substrate. It will feed on a variety of both live and dead animal foods and fruit. Efforts should be made to breed these lizards in captivity. Females lack the well-developed femoral pores of males. Photo by Jim Bridges and Bob Prince.©

A green or Chinese water dragon (*Physignathus cocincinus*). This semi-arboreal species is easily kept in a tropical vivarium with orchid bark or a soil substrate. It feeds on insects, dead animal foods and some fruit or other plant matter. They are easily bred if kept in pairs or trios. Photo by Jim Bridges and Bob Prince.©

A pair of green or double-crested basilisk *(Basiliscus plumifrons)*. Except for its size, this is the most dragonlike of all the lizards. Males with their cranial, dorsal and caudal crests are like creatures out of a fanstasy; they also have gorgeous colors. They require large tropical vivaria with cork rounds or thick branches at an angle for climbing. One negative characteristic of this species as a captive is its tendency for skittish flight behaviors, running into the sides of their vivaria and bashing their snouts. Fortunately, they are now bred by the hundreds and captive-hatched/-raised animals are significantly calmer than their wild relatives. Insects, small mice, and occasional fruit are relished by this voracious species. Photo by Jim Bridges and Bob Prince.©

A Parson's chameleon *(Chamaeleo parsonii)*. This Malagasy species is the largest of the true chameleons. Not particularly difficult to keep if one starts with young animals; keep them in large, well-ventilated enclosures, with temperatures not too warm (in the mid to high 70's (25 to 26°C) with low 80's (28.9 to 30°C) at the warmest). In the winter established specimens will tolerate night temperatures in the 50's (10 to 15°C) with no problems. Moderate relative humidity and a water drip will also be required. Efforts should be made to successfully and consistently breed this species in captivity before it becomes unavailable. Do not handle except when necessary. One of the most extraordinary of the reptiles. Photo by Jim Bridges and Bob Prince.©

A sandfish *(Scincus scincus)*. A fossorial (burrowing) skink that will spend most of its time in a dry sand with warm daytime temperatures. It requires a desert vivarium and can be kept with other desert species in the same size range. All members of the genus *Scincus* are live-bearing. Photo by Jim Bridges and Bob Prince.©

A Schneider's skink *(Eumeces schneideri)*. This North African-to-Central Asian species has been regularly available in recent years. Attractive, docile and hardy, it should be kept in a large desert vivarium with a sand substrate. They require warm daytime temperatures. They will feed on both live and dead animal foods, including high quality canned dog food. A large humidified shelter is recommended. They enjoy a light morning misting. Males should not be kept together. Males can be recognized by their larger heads, somewhat larger size and brighter coloration. Egg-laying. Photo by Jim Bridges and Bob Prince.©

The Sudan plated lizard of the pet trade (*Gerrhosaurus major*). This is a medium-size, hardy species, highly recommended for beginners or for those who want a lizard pet. They feed on both live and dead animal food, as well as some fruit. Some have a high contrast pattern while others are more dull. Generally underappreciated because it is not as flashy as other species, yet it has a nice personality. Like all *Gerrhosaurus*, this species lays eggs. Photo by Jim Bridges and Bob Prince.©

A leopard gecko (*Eublepharis macularius*). This species, originally imported from Pakistan, is now well established in the herpetocultural trade. It is one of the hardiest and easiest to keep of all lizards. Photo by Jim Bridges and Bob Prince.©

A gold dust day gecko (*Phelsuma laticauda*). In recent years, a wide selection of Malagasy day geckos has become available to herpetoculturists. These are the jewels of the lizard world. Most species will thrive in planted tropical vivaria and will breed readily. The gold dust day gecko is one of the easiest to breed of the group. They will feed on both insects and soft fruit/banana or peach baby food. Photo by Jim Bridges and Bob Prince.[©]

A *Japalura* species. These semi-arboreal/arboreal species have occasionally been imported in recent years. They should be kept in tropical vivaria with moderately high relative humidity. Photo by Jim Bridges and Bob Prince.[©]

A crevice spiny lizard (*Sceloporus poinsetti*). This live-bearing species should be kept in a desert vivarium with extensive rock work. The daytime temperature should be high with a significant night drop of 8 to 15°F (4.4 to 8.3°C). Some exposure to natural sunlight is recommended. They should be cooled in the winter. As with all spiny lizards, check for mites and parasites. In addition to insects, they will eat some plant matter. Photo by Jim Bridges and Bob Prince.[©]

A Drakensberg crag lizard *(Pseudocordylus melanotus subviridis)*. Members of this genus are occasionally available. Like members of the genus *Cordylus*, they should be kept in desert vivaria. They are live bearers. Photo by Jim Bridges and Bob Prince.©

An inland bearded dragon *(Pogona vitticeps)*. This is one of the most personable and popular of the insect-eating lizards. Photo by Corey Blanc.

Yarrow's spiny lizard *(Sceloporus jarrovii)*. This is an unusually attractive member of the species. Care is similar to that of the crevice spiny lizard. Photo by Jim Bridges and Bob Prince.©

General Guidelines for the Herpetoculture of Some of the More Popular Insect-Eating Lizard Species

Note: These are very general guidelines. It is recommended that you purchase any available literature which addresses in detail the needs of the lizard species you intend to keep.

Eublepharidae
(Geckos with movable eyelids)
Sexing: Males have hemipenile bulges and enlarged pre-anal pores.

The eublepharids are geckos with movable eyelids and lacking pads of lamellae at the ends of their digits. They are all terrestrial with the exception of *Aeluroscalabotes*, which is semi-arboreal. The leopard gecko *(Eublepharis macularius)* and the African fat-tail gecko *(Hemitheconyx caudicinctus)* are the most readily available. They can be maintained in desert vivaria with both dry and humidified shelters. A damp sand/soil area should be available for egg laying. African fat-tail geckos have also been successfully maintained on orchid bark. Daytime temperatures should be in the low 80's°F (26.7 to 28.3°C) and nighttime temperatures can drop into the 70's°F (21 to 26°C). Leopard geckos will tolerate nighttime temperatures in the 60's°F (15.6 to 20.6°C) during the winter. A slight drop of 5 to 7°F (2.8 to 3.9°C) in winter temperature, along with a photoperiod reduction, is recommended for fat-tail geckos. Breeding groups should consist of one male with several females. Both species will breed readily and lay several clutches of two eggs each year. North American desert banded geckos *(Coleonyx)* can be kept under conditions similar to leopard geckos, but their diet will have to be adjusted to their small size. Winter cooling is recommended for breeding the desert *Coleonyx*.

Tropical *Coleonyx* should be kept in tropical vivaria on orchid bark or a potting soil/orchid bark mix. They should be kept at temperatures in the high 70's to low 80's°F (25 to 28.3°C). A moist substrate should be available for egg laying. The attractive Central American banded gecko (*Coleonyx mitratus*) is now being bred in increasing numbers in the United States.

Gekkonidae
(Geckos with immovable eyelids)

Special requirements: All geckos require high calcium levels in their diet, particularly during the breeding season. As a broad rule (there are many exceptions), geckos are among the easiest to keep of the lizards.

Sexing: Most male geckos have pronounced hemipenile bulges. In many species, males also have enlarged pre-anal or femoral pores.

Frog-eyed geckos *(Teratoscincus)* can be maintained as leopard geckos are, though they do appreciate an opportunity to bask, particularly at the end of the day (thus, a low-wattage red light/basking area should be made available). Some herpetoculturists supply frog-eyed geckos with a BL blacklight, because it may be beneficial for successful breeding. Breeding success depends on calcium availability, and temperatures into the low 60's°F (15.6 to 20.6°C) at night, combined with a reduced winter photoperiod. These are some of the most beautiful of the terrestrial geckos (particularly *T. keyzerlingii*) and efforts should be made to breed them more consistently.

Gecko species *(G. gekko, G. vittatus,* etc.), house geckos, and flying geckos *(Ptychozoon)* should be kept in tropical vivaria. They are generally easy to keep and breed, but imports should be checked and treated for internal parasites.

Bent-toed geckos *(Cyrtodactylus)* are generally considered somewhat difficult. They should be kept in tropical vivaria with moderate-to-high relative humidity. Orchid bark is an adequate substrate; so is a peat-moss-based potting spoil. Shelters should be provided, as well as climbing areas. The temperatures should be moderate (in the mid 70's to low 80's°F (23.3 to 28.3°C) during the day, in the low to mid 70's°F (21 to 26°C) at night). Imports should be treated for internal parasites. Once established, certain species, such as *Cyrtodactylus pulchellus,* can be quite hardy. More efforts should be made to establish these species in captivity.

Day geckos *(Phelsuma)* are now imported in large numbers from the Malagasy Republic. They are some of the jewels of the lizard world. Many of the species are very hardy, adaptable and among the easiest to keep of the lizards. The giant day gecko *(Phelsuma madagascariensis grandis)* and several of the dwarf day geckos *(Phelsuma laticauda, Phelsuma lineata, Phelsuma quadriocellata, Phelsuma serraticauda)* are recommended for beginners. Most of these lizards will fare well in planted tropical vivaria at temperatures in the high 70's to mid 80's°F (25 to 28.3°C). They are primarily insect-eaters but also relish soft fruit and fruit baby foods. Water should be provided through misting. Many species are easy to breed. See McKeown (1993) for details on their herpetoculture. Most species should be kept in single pairs; others can be kept in small colonies in large vivaria. Females lay several clutches of two eggs each year.

Madagascar velvet geckos *(Homopholis)* can be kept and bred under conditions similar to those required by day geckos. They should be kept in single pairs.

Moorish and white-spotted geckos *(Tarentola mauritanica, Tarentola annularis)*, fan-footed geckos *(Ptyodactylus hasselquistii)*, *Stenodactylus* species and microgeckos *(Tropiocolotes)* should be kept in desert vivaria with rock work, dried wood sections, and/or cork bark. A section of moist substrate or a humidified shelter should be available. Vertical rock areas or sections of cork bark should be created for *Tarentola* and *Ptyodactylus*.

Anguidae
(Legless lizards, alligator lizards, galliwasps)
There are relatively few anguid species available in the pet trade. United States alligator lizards *(Gerrhonotus)* are uncommon or protected; thus, they are seldom available in the pet trade. This genus has been neglected by United States herpetoculturists. Most species are easy to maintain in a vivarium with a sand/moss/soil mix, with one half of the vivarium kept dampened. Shelter and climbing areas of cork bark are recommended. They enjoy temperatures in the high 70's to low 80's°F (25 to 28.3°C) during the day, with a 10°F (5.5°C) temperature drop at night. During the winter, they should be hibernated with daytime temperatures in the 60's°F (15.6 to 20.6°C) and nighttime temperatures in the 50's°F (10 to 15°C). They will breed readily in the spring and will usually lay multiple clutches. They are primarily insect-eating. Water

should be available at all times. A common cause of death in captivity is keeping these animals too warm and too dry.

The Scheltopuzik or European giant legless lizard can be kept under similar conditions. The slow worm *(Anguis fragilis)* requires a damper substrate with a higher percentage of potting soil. Daily misting is recommended. Winter hibernation temperatures should be 45 to 50°F (7.2 to 10°C). Scheltopuziks feed on insects, small rodents, lean meat and dog food.

The American legless lizards *(Ophisaurus)* can be kept under conditions similar to alligator lizards, except that they like warmer daytime temperatures of 80 to 86°F (26.7 to 30°C) and warmer nighttime temperatures in the 70's°F (21 to 26°C). Winter cooling in the 60's°F (15.6 to 20.6°C) is adequate.

Chameleonidae
Agaminae
Agamines are widely distributed Old World lizards that have successfully colonized a wide variety of habitats.

Agama species live primarily in arid-to-semi-arid areas; thus, they should be kept in desert vivaria with rock work and climbing areas. Many species do not fare well in captivity because they are specialized for feeding on ants. Others are more generalized feeders and adapt better to captivity. A basking area which reaches a temperature of 90 to 100°F (32.2 to 37.8°C) should be provided. Many *Agama* species eat some vegetable matter, particularly flower petals. Exposure to sunlight is recommended.

Green water dragons *(Physignathus cocincinus)* and sailfin lizards *(Hydrosaurus)* are some of the largest agamine lizards. They require large tropical vivaria with a sizeable water area. The water dragons are primarily insectivorous but they also eat small mammals, dead animal foods (such as dog food), and some vegetable matter. The sailfin lizards have dietary requirements similar to water dragons, except that they become more vegetarian by the time they are adults. Both are egg-layers and do breed in captivity. Green water dragons can be kept in groups of one male and several females, but sailfin lizards should only be kept as single pairs.

The Australian *Pogona* species, known in the trade as bearded dragons, are among the most popular of the lizards. The inland bearded dragon *(Pogona vitticeps)* is the most readily available species. Several thousand are bred annually by hobbyists in the United States. They should be kept in desert vivaria with climbing areas of rock or cork rounds or dried wood sections. They are insectivorous but also eat vegetable matter, including fruit, kale and flower petals. Twice weekly brief exposure to sunlight is recommended, particularly when raising juveniles. Sexing can be done through manual eversion of the hemipenes and through sexually dimorphic characteristics, including a relatively larger head and the presence of enlarged femoral and pre-anal pores in males. They breed readily and lay several clutches of up to twenty eggs per breeding season.

Chameleoninae (True chameleons)

Sexing: Males have hemipenile bulges; there are also sexually dimorphic characteristics such as size, color and enlarged helmets or ornaments in males.

These are some of the most beautiful and fascinating of all the lizards, as well as the most frustrating to keep alive. One thing to realize is that many of the egg-laying species are naturally short-lived. Another is that many wild-collected animals arrive infested with parasites. The best course for being successful is to buy captive-bred animals with requirements that you can easily meet.

In the author's opinion the following (ranked in order of hardiness) are among the easiest to keep of the chameleons:

1. Natal midland dwarf chameleon *(Bradypodion thamnobates)*. This is a small live-bearing species which is being bred and becoming available in increasing numbers.

2. Veiled chameleon *(Chamaeleo calyptratus)*. This species is currently bred, possibly numbering in the thousands, by United States herpetoculturists.

3. Panther chameleon *(Chamaeleo pardalis)*. This species is captive bred in moderate numbers.

The key with chameleons is to initially start with juvenile animals and to provide tall enclosures, a high-quality insect diet offered daily, daily misting and/or a water-drip system, climbing areas, plants for shade, occasional exposure to natural sunlight (always provide shade), moderate relative humidity and the right temperature range. Some of the dwarf chameleons *(Rhampholeon* and *Brookesia)* are actually quite hardy and will fare well indoors if maintained at temperatures in the 70's°F (21 to 26°C). The popular Jackson's chameleon is only recommended if you can provide the cool temperatures it prefers (in the 70's°F (21 to 26°C) during the day (maximum of low 80's°F (26.7 to 28.3°C)) and into the 60's°F (15.6 to 20.6°C) or even the 50's°F (10 to 15°C) at night, plus an opportunity for exposure to some sunlight (always with a shaded section available). All true chameleons are primarily insect-eating though some, such as the veiled chameleon *(Chamaeleo calyptratus),* will also eat some plant matter.

Most chameleon species are egg-laying. Some African montane and cooler climate species are live-bearing (i.e., Jackson's chameleons and the Natal dwarf chameleon *(Bradypodion thamnobates)).* Generally, true chameleons are recommended for more experienced herpetoculturists (with the exception of some of the hardy species mentioned earlier). Ongoing research with these species will, however, lead to information and methods that will one day facilitate their herpetoculture.

Cordylidae
Cordylinae (Girdled-tailed lizards)
Members of the girdle-tailed *(Cordylus),* false girdle-tailed *(Pseudocordylus)* and flat lizards *(Platysaurus)* are hardy animals that should be set up in large desert vivaria with rock work. Temperatures in the day should be in the 80's°F (26.7 to 31.7°C) with a basking spot. Nighttime temperatures should drop 10 to 15°F (5.5 to 7.7°C). By manipulating the temperature and photoperiod, many of these lizards do breed. Use a cooling regimen a few degrees colder than that used for subtropical lizards. These are among the hardiest of the lizards to keep in captivity. Some species are very colorful. They are live bearing, except for *Platysaurus* (usually 1 to 4 young). Because of relatively low reproductive rates, these species could be impacted by unmanaged commercial collecting. They are not recommended for handling.

Gerrhosaurines (Plated lizards)

Members of the genus *Gerrhosaurus* (African) will do well in a desert/dry-forest-type vivarium. The substrate should be dry except for one moistened area (soil/sand/orchid bark mix) in a pan buried flush with the dry substrate. Generally African plated lizards are hardy and easy to keep. They are egg-layers.

Members of the genus *Zonosaurus* (Malagasy) can be kept in a vivarium with a soil/sand/fine orchid bark mixture as a substrate. Half of the substrate in the enclosure should be kept dry and half should be kept slightly moist. Success has also been had keeping *Zonosaurus* species on orchid bark and with some species, such as *Z. quadrilineatus*, on sand. The larger species are easier to keep than the smaller ones. Males have large femoral pores. They are egg-layers.

Corythophanidae

Basilisks (*Basiliscus*). Three species are regularly available in the trade; *B. basiliscus*, *B. plumifrons* and *B. vittatus*. The first two species mentioned are bred in some numbers in captivity. They require large tropical vivaria. Because of their arboreal habits, plants should be provided. They need large water containers and shelters in the form of sections of cork tube. They are easy to breed. The biggest problem is skittish flight behavior, sometimes leading to smashed snouts. Males should be kept separately. Egg-laying, with usually 2 to 3 clutches per year.

Helmeted iguanid or forest chameleon (*Corythophanes cristatus*). This neat arboreal species tends to be difficult in the long term and is not recommended for beginners. It requires a warm, planted tropical vivarium with branches or cork rounds, moderately high relative humidity and adequate ventilation. Imports should be treated for parasites. These animals should not be handled except when necessary. A drip watering system is a good idea. They are insectivorous and egg-laying.

Crotaphytidae
(North American collared lizards and leopard lizards)

North American collared lizards (*Crotaphytus*). These lizards will fare well in large desert vivaria. Temperatures during the day should be in the 80's°F (26.7 to 31.7°C) with a basking spot in the 90's°F (32.2 to 37.2°C) at the area closest to the light. Night temperatures can drop into the 60's°F (15.6 to 20.6°C) during most of the year and into the 50's°F (10 to 15°C) during the winter. Rocks and shelters and areas for climbing, such as section of cork round are recommended. These lizards are diggers so care must be given to protect the bases of plants when designing a naturalistic vivarium. Rocks must also be anchored firmly. These attractive lizards are now being captive-bred in small numbers in the United States. Captive-bred animals are very adaptable and tame lizards which many consider personable. These lizards are egg-layers and will breed readily with winter cooling and reduced photoperiod.

Lacertidae

Sexing: Males typically have enlarged femoral pores. Lacertids may also be sexually dimorphic, the males often being larger, with larger heads and, in some cases, brighter coloration.

Most of the imported lacertids (*Acanthodactylus, Lacerta, Podarcis*) from Europe and North Africa will fare best in desert-type vivaria with rock work and shelters. If kept too damp, some species will develop a skin disease which will often prove fatal. Some of the most impressive species are the eyed or jewel lacerta (*Lacerta lepida*) and the green lacerta (*Lacerta viridis*). They are best kept in groups of one male with several females. The larger species may attack other lizards, particularly males, during breeding. Otherwise, many of the species are quite hardy and entertaining vivarium animals. They are primarily insectivorous, though they do eat some plant matter/soft fruit. *Lacerta* and *Podarcis* breed readily following winter cooling. Egg-laying except for the viviparous lizard (*Lacerta vivipara*).

Long-tailed grass lizards (*Takydromus*) are the only regularly imported Asian lacertids. They will fare best in a half-dry, half-moist vivarium with a substrate of orchid bark and potting soil. Provide twigs and low plants for climbing. Small 1-to-2 week old crickets should be offered as food. Water in a shallow container should be available at <u>all</u> times. They should be kept in the high 70's°F (25 to 26°C) with a low-wattage basking light. Night temperatures can drop into the 60's°F (15.6 to 20.6°C). They are egg-laying.

Opluridae
(Malagasy iguanids)
Most available species are members of the genus *Oplurus*, notably *O. cuvieri* and *O. cyclurus*. They are best kept in desert vivaria with some rock work, and possibly a section of cholla, dry wood or cork. Unlike many other lizard species, they do not autotomize (drop) their tails. They are primarily insectivorous. Egg-layers, usually with small clutches (4 to 6 eggs) laid between rocks.

Phrynosomatidae
Horned lizards *(Phrynosoma)*. Most species available in the United States pet trade are difficult to keep alive for an extended period of time, in part because of their specialized ant diet. They are best left to specialists until systems are developed for long-term success. For several species, mealworms have proven a better alternate food than crickets. These lizards should be offered water regularly, orally with an eye dropper or pipette releasing droplets of water at the tips of their snouts. They should be kept in desert vivaria; better yet, in outdoor vivaria if the weather allows it.

Spiny lizards *(Sceloporus)* are the most readily available of the phrynosomatids. Most of the United States species offered in the trade can be kept in desert vivaria with rock and wood in the landscape. They require warm temperatures during the day with a significant drop at night. Winter cooling is required for breeding. Primarily insectivorous, they will also eat plant matter. Exposure to sunlight is recommended. *Sceloporus* includes egg-laying and live-bearing species. Occasionally imported from Central America, the emerald swift *(Sceloporus malachitus)* fares better in a tropical vivarium with cork sections to climb on.

Polychridae
Sexing: Males have hemipenile bulges. In anoles, males are often larger, with larger heads and dewlaps.

Anoles *(Anolis)* are among the most popular species, particularly the green anole. They fare well in planted tropical vivaria, with branches and climbing areas provided for most species. Some species live on bark, others more at ground level. Relative humidity requirements vary somewhat between species.

Most species are arboreal, requiring branches for climbing. They are insect-eating but also eat banana baby food and certain soft fruit. They are best kept in groups of one male with several females. Water should be provided through misting or a water-drip system. They are egg-laying, typically with one egg per clutch.

Scincidae
(Skinks)

Sexing: In some species sexual dimorphism, including larger head size and coloration, and broader tail base in males, can be used for sexing. In others, manual eversion of the hemipenes (if applied carefully) will often prove effective. Some skinks are simply difficult to sex.

Skinks number over 1,000 species and are probably the most abundant of the lizards. It is not possible to make broad generalizations for this group. As a rule, skinks from forests with moist soils should be kept in a forest floor vivarium, with a burrowing medium consisting of a soil/fine orchid bark/sand mixture. Cork sections for shelters and as climbing areas should be provided. Skinks from desert areas usually fare well on sand. Provide rock and sections of bark for climbing and basking. Some desert-burrowing species, such as the sandfish *(Scincus)* and many of the barrel skinks *(Chalcides)*, only fare well if kept on sand. Sexing can be difficult with many species, although manual eversion of the hemipenes often works if applied gently.

In addition to insects, many of the small-to-medium skinks will feed on dog food, as well as some fruits and vegetables. Some of the larger skinks, such as the prehensile-tailed skink, are primarily vegetarian.

Teiidae
(Ameivas, tegus, whiptails and racerunners)

Ameivas are occasionally imported in some numbers as are certain tropical *Cnemidophorus.* They are best kept in large vivaria with a thick layer of a sand/peat moss or sand/potting soil mix, which is slightly dampened and patted down, so that it is cohesive enough to allow for the digging of burrows. A good alternative is to insert sections of PVC pipe at an angle in the substrate. One section should contain a mulch or a pile of leaves for them to burrow in. These species like warm (85°F)

(29.4°C) daytime temperatures. A spotlight should be provided, as well as some diversity of landscape through rock work, or preferably sections of wood or cork. The relative humidity for tropical species should be around 70%. The vivarium should have good ventilation. BL-type blacklights are recommended and, if possible, a source of UV-B, either sunlight, mercury lamp or UV-B fluorescent bulbs. These lizards are insectivorous, but will also feed on lean meats strips. They will also eat some soft fruit and cooked mashed vegetables. Desert teiids are best kept in desert vivaria with shelters and dry leaf piles. Sunlight or another UV-B source is highly recommended.

Varanidae
(Monitor lizards)
This book is only concerned with the smaller insect-eating varanids.

At the time of writing, Timor monitors *(Varanus timorensis)*, and green *(Varanus prasinus)* and black *(Varanus beccari)* tree monitors are occasionally available in the pet trade. They must be examined and treated for internal parasites, particularly protozoans. These are all arboreal species which should be kept in tropical vivaria with moderately high relative humidity. Cork rounds or thick branches should be provided for climbing. Cork rounds are an excellent shelter for these species. Timor monitors will breed readily in captivity. They should be kept in groups of one male with several females in very large vivaria. In small poorly designed vivaria, these monitors will ruin their snouts. Sexing is often best determined by observation of their behaviors. Diet should be primarily insectivorous, with occasional feeding of larger pink mice. The larger tropical forest Indonesian species of monitors can be kept under more or less similar conditions, except that landscape features and diet must be adjusted to their size, e.g., offer fuzzy-to-just-weaned mice instead of large pink mice.

An Overview of the Lizards

Iguania

1. **[Family] Chamaeleonidae:**
    a. **[Subfamily] Agaminae:** Agamas, water dragons, bearded dragons
    b. **Chamaeleoninae:** True chameleons
    c. **Leiolepidinae:** Butterfly agamas, Uromastyx

2. **Corythophanidae:** Basilisks, helmeted iguanid *(Corythophanes)*

3. **Crotaphytidae:** Collared lizards, leopard lizard

4. **Hoplocercidae:** Club-tailed iguanids

5. **Iguanidae:** Iguanas, chuckwallas

6. **Opluridae:** Madagascar iguanids

7. **Phrynosomatidae:** Horned lizards *(Phrynosoma)*

8. **Polychridae:** Anoles, prehensile-tailed lizards *(Polychrus)*

9. **Tropiduridae:**
    a. **Leiocephalinae:** Curly-tailed lizards *(Leiocephalus)*
    b. **Liolaeminae:** Chilean or South American swifts
    c. **Tropidurinae:** Lava lizards *(Tropidurus)*

Gekkota

1. **Eublepharidae:** Geckos with movable eyelids

2. **Gekkonidae:** Geckos with immovable eyelids

Autarchoglossa

1. **Anguidae:** Legless lizards, alligator lizards, galliwasps

2. **Cordylidae:**
   Cordylinae: Girdle-tailed lizards
   Gerrhosaurinae: Plated lizards

3. **Dibamidae:**

4. **Gymnothalmidae:**

5. **Helodermatidae:** Gila monster, beaded lizards

6. **Lacertidae:** Lacertas

7. **Scincidae:**
   a. **Acontiinae:** South African limbless skinks
   b. **Feylinae:** Central African limbless skinks
   c. **Lygosominae:** Predominantly Australasian skinks
   d. **Scincinae:** Predominantly African-Eurasian skinks

8. **Teiidae:** Ameivas, tegus, whiptail lizards

9. **Varanidae:** Monitor lizards

10. **Xantusidae:** Night lizards *(Xantusia), Lepidophyma*

11. **Xenosauridae:** Crocodile lizards, xenosaurs

Source Materials & Recommended Reading

Alberts, A. 1994. Ultraviolet Light and Lizards: More than Meets the Eye. The Vivarium Vol. 5 No. 4 p 24-28. *Recommended reading for anyone trying to figure out what the UV-A and UV-B issue is all about.*

De Vosjoli, P. 1992. The General Care and Maintenance of Green Anoles. Advanced Vivarium Systems, Inc., Lakeside, CA.

De Vosjoli, P. 1992. The General Care and Maintenance of Green Water Dragons, Basilisks and Sailfin Lizards. Advanced Vivarium Systems, Inc., Lakeside, CA.

De Vosjoli, P. and R. Mailloux. 1993. The General Care and Maintenance of Bearded Dragons. Advanced Vivarium Systems, Inc., Lakeside, CA.

Frost, D.R. and R. Etheridge. 1989. A Phylogenetic Analysis and Taxonomy of Iguanian Lizards. Misc. Pub. No. 81 Univ. of Kansas, Museum of Natural History, Lawrence, KS. *This work has generated quite a bit of controversy among taxonomists but the methodology and taxonomic analysis are of the highest standards.*

Frye, F. 1991. Reptile Care. Volume 1 and 2. T.F.H. *This expensive 2-volume set is the veterinary standard for diagnosing and treating reptile diseases. The experienced hobbyist will find it invaluable. Others will find it too technical, particularly the second volume.*

Frye, F. 1993. Reptile Clinician's Handbook. Krieger Publishing, Malabar, FL. *For the hobbyist, this small-format wire-bound book is a lot more user friendly and economical than the large 2-volume set. It does lack photos that can prove invaluable in helping the inexperienced hobbyist diagnose a lizard's condition. Metabolic bone disease, one of the most common problems in captive reptiles, is only briefly mentioned in this abridged work.*

Gehrmann, W.H. 1994. Spectral Characteristics of Lamps Commonly Used in Herpetoculture. The Vivarium Vol. 5 No. 5 p 16-21. *A great article for anyone interested in lighting and reptile care. Highly recommended.*

Klingenberg, R. 1993. Understanding Reptile Parasites. Advanced Vivarium Systems, Inc., Lakeside, CA. *What every serious herpetoculturist should know about reptile parasites. Highly recommended.*

Marquardt, K., M. Levine and M. La Rochelle. 1993. Animal Scam: The Beastly Abuse of Human Rights. Regnery Gateway, Washington D.C. *Recommended for anyone interested in some of the real scoop about animal rights organizations. This book exposes the not-so-ethical side of the people who are actively trying to segregate non-human consciousness from human consciousness and put an end to the keeping of animals in captivity.*

Mattison, C. 1991. Keeping and Breeding Lizards. Blandford. London, distributed by Sterling, New York. *Chris has put together a well written overview of lizards and their herpetoculture.*

McKeown, S. 1993. The General Care and Maintenance of Day Geckos. Advanced Vivarium Systems, Inc., Lakeside, CA. *The standard English language reference on the herpetoculture of these popular lizards.*

Zimmerman, E. 1986. Breeding Terrarium Animals. T.F.H. *An invaluable reference on keeping and breeding amphibians and reptiles. A gem of a book that should be in every lizard keeper's library. T.F.H. has recently published this book with a new cover and title. Look for the author's name.*

Zug G.R. 1993. Herpetology: An introductory biology of amphibians and reptiles. Academic Press, Inc. San Diego, CA . *A very readable and informative introduction to herpetology. Basic information most herpetoculturists and amateur herpetologists should know.*

Publications

There are several herpetocultural magazines on the market. Each has its own perspective and unique approach to presenting information. We've come a long way in the past seven years.

Reptile and Amphibian Magazine, RD 3, Box 3709-A, Pottsville, Pennsylvania 17901

Reptiles, PO Box 58700, Boulder, CO 80322

The Reptilian Magazine, Mantella Publishing, 22 Firs Close, Hazlemere, High Wycombe, Bucks HP 15 7TF, Great Britain

The Vivarium, PO Box 300067, Escondido, California 92030

Some herpetological societies publish sizeable and informative publications. Some have an intersociety newsletter exchange program. Examine newsletters and bulletins of other societies to discover those to which you would like to subscribe. One of the most popular and informative of the herpetological society publications is:

Bulletin of the Chicago Herpetological Society, 2001 North Clark Street, Chicago, Illinois 60614

Products

Note: The author has chosen not to list the addresses of manufacturers listed in this manual: first, because most do not sell direct to the public; and secondly, because the products are available through retail sources, either stores or mail-order. Check the advertisers in herpetocultural magazines for sources.

Enclosures
Stay-In Reptile: Screen-top and screen-side glass enclosures.
Vivarium Research Group: (954) 984-0031. Sliding-glass-front enclosures.

Lights
Spectra Lite®: Full spectrum fluorescent bulbs. Replace every 6-12 months for full efficiency.
Vita Lite®: Full spectrum fluorescent bulbs. Replace every 6-12 months for full efficiency.
Chromalux incandescent bulbs: Claims to be full spectrum, but at the time of writing the neodymium-coated bulbs do not generate much UV-A or UV-B compared with fluorescent full-spectrum bulbs. The manufacturing company, Luminar, is said to have a UV-B-generating bulb.
UV-B bulbs: Two companies, Fluker's and ZooMed®, are promoting UV-generating bulbs, including UV-B, to be available in the near future.

Thermostats
Custom Reptile Network®: A thermostatic system that allows for day/night programming.
Microclimate Electronix®: Pulse-proportional thermostats.
Similar thermostats are nowbeing offered by other companies.
Desa® International, Bowling Green, Kentucky: Forced-air heater thermostats.

Thermometers
Radio Shack stores: A good source for relatively inexpensive good quality digital thermometers.
Edmund Scientific (Phone:609-573-6250): The author has tried several of the digital thermometers in their catalog; batteries had to be replaced frequently.
Sunbeam®: Offers some high quality digital thermometers when you can find them.

Hygrometers
Edmund Scientific: One source for digital hygrometers, but a little bit of inquiry should lead you to other sources.

Scales
Edmund Scientific: A good source for some relatively inexpensive yet accurate digital scales.

Heating equipment
FlexWatt®
Tetra Terrafauna®
Tropic Zone®
Ultratherm®
ZooMed®
Note: There are others on the market and there are more due in the future.

Vitamin/mineral supplements
Mardel Laboratories: Produces vitamin/mineral supplements and some reptile health products.
Nekton®: Produces a range of reptile vitamins. Some, including Nekton Rep, may have too much vitamin A for some lizards.
TetraTerrafauna®: Produces a wide range of reptile food, health and nutrition products.
ZooMed®: Produces Reptivite®, a powdered vitamin/mineral supplement popular among lizard keepers, as well as reptile foods and health products.

Calcium/D3 Supplements
Nekton®: Nekton MSA is a calcium/vitamin D3 supplement (with other minerals) that adheres well to crickets.
Rep Cal®: Oyster shell calcium and vitamin D3 supplement. A popular and readily available calcium/vitamin D3 source.

Calcium carbonate
This is sometimes available in feed stores under the name of limestone flour. It should be more readily available in the reptile trade under simply calcium carbonate or oyster shell calcium.

Note: These lists reflect the author's information base and are not meant to imply product preference. An updated edition of this book will be published in the future. If you want your product(s) to be considered for listing, send informative printed product brochures to:

American Federation of Herpetoculturists
Lizard Keeper's Update
Post Office Box 300067
Escondido, California 92030-0067

Index